TRAUNER VERLAG
BILDUNG
Bildung, die begeistert!

Englisch für die Berufsreifeprüfung – Hauptmodul

GABRIELE RAAB
CHRISTINA KODRÉ

Forms and Structures

Impressum

Raab u. a., Englisch für die Berufsreifeprüfung – Hauptmodul
■ Forms and Structures
3. Auflage 2020
TRAUNER Verlag, Linz

Die Autorinnen

MAG. GABRIELE RAAB
Freiberufliche Trainerin für Sprachen; Trainerin an Erwachsenenbildungseinrichtungen (Schwerpunkt Berufsreifeprüfung)

MAG. CHRISTINA KODRÉ
Trainerin an einer Erwachsenenbildungseinrichtung (Schwerpunkt Berufsreifeprüfung); HTL Leonding

Dieses Lehrwerk wurde auf der Grundlage des kompetenzbasierten Curriculums Englisch für die Berufsreifeprüfung erstellt und richtet sich nach dem aktuellen Leitfaden für die BRP Englisch; die Auswahl und die Gewichtung der Inhalte erfolgt durch die Lehrenden bzw. Trainerinnen und Trainer.

Lektorat/Produktmanagement:
Mag. Katharina Stadler
Titelgestaltung: Bettina Victor
Gestaltung und Grafik: Klara Jedinger
Schulbuchvergütung/Bildrechte:
© Bildrecht GmbH/Wien
Gesamtherstellung:
Vorarlberger Verlagsanstalt GmbH
Schwefel 81, 6850 Dornbirn

ISBN 978-3-99062-735-8
www.trauner.at

Vorwort

Der vorliegende Band **„Forms and Structures"** wurde für den Unterricht im **Hauptmodul** zur **Berufsreifeprüfung** bzw. **Lehre mit Matura aus Englisch** entwickelt. Zusammen mit dem Band **„Topics"** dient er der umfassenden Vorbereitung auf die Berufsmatura.

Mit übersichtlichen, nach grammatischen Schwerpunkten gegliederten Kapiteln und einer Fülle von dazu passenden Übungsaufgaben können **bestehende Kenntnisse und Fertigkeiten im Satzbau und in der Grammatik** auf dem **Niveau B2** erweitert und auf **Maturaniveau** gebracht werden. Die einzelnen Kapitel sind alphabetisch geordnet. Sie bieten zusätzlich Übungen, bei denen die Kursteilnehmer/innen die gelernten Inhalte in einem situativen Kontext anwenden sollen. Diese Texte sind auf die im „Topics"-Band behandelten Themenkreise abgestimmt. Dadurch wird das Gelernte gefestigt und die Anwendung im Kontext ermöglicht.

Sollte der letzte Englischunterricht schon einige Jahre zurückliegen, bieten die beiden Bände **„Topics and Language in Use"** und **„Workbook" des Basismoduls** eine optimale Möglichkeit, bereits verblasste Kenntnisse in kurzer Zeit aufzufrischen, verloren Geglaubtes zu aktivieren und wieder mehr Sicherheit im Gebrauch der englischen Sprache zu erlangen. Sie sind bezüglich Themen und Wortschatz auf die Bände des Hauptmoduls abgestimmt und erleichtern den Einstieg.

Das sprachliche Niveau entspricht **B2** des Gemeinsamen Europäischen Referenzrahmens für Sprachen (GERS). Die Rechtschreibung orientiert sich grundsätzlich an der modernen britischen Schreibweise.

Zu diesem Band gibt es einen **eSquirrel-Kurs** mit 500 Übungsbeispielen. Damit können Sie Ihre Grammatik-Kenntnisse auch ganz bequem unterwegs am Smartphone oder Tablet vertiefen.

eSquirrel
Lernen wird mobil
www.esquirrel.at/trauner

Wesentliche Elemente und verwendete Symbole

Die angeführten **Ziele** kennzeichnen, über welche **Kompetenzen** die Lernenden nach der Bearbeitung des jeweiligen Kapitels verfügen. Sie orientieren sich am aktuellen **kompetenzbasierten Curriculum Englisch** für die Berufsreifeprüfung und sind **leitfadenkonform.**

Meine Ziele

Nach Bearbeitung dieses Kapitels kann ich

- Ziel 1;
- Ziel 2;
- Ziel 3.

Zur Erarbeitung der Kenntnisse und Fertigkeiten sowie zur Kontrolle des Lernerfolgs stehen den Lernenden unterschiedliche **Arbeitsaufgaben** und umfassende **Arbeitsaufträge** („Ziele erreicht?") zur Verfügung, die sich ebenfalls am kompetenzorientierten Curriculum orientieren. Im Mittelpunkt steht hier die **praktische Anwendung** der erarbeiteten Inhalte des jeweiligen Kapitels.

Schriftliche Aufgabenstellungen (Your Turn):

Your Turn

Your Turn 1

Your Turn 2

...

„Ziele erreicht?"-Aufgaben am Ende jedes Kapitels zeigen den Kompetenzzuwachs in der Anwendung des Grammatikkapitels auf:

Ziele erreicht?

Challenge 1

Challenge 2

...

Folgende weitere Piktogramme unterstützen das Lehren und Lernen mit dem Buch:

für Wissenswertes und Tipps

für „Achtung!" oder „Beachte!"

für Verweise auf andere Bände

Wir wünschen Ihnen ein spannendes Lernen sowie viel Erfolg beim Anwenden der erworbenen Sprachkompetenzen!

Die Autorinnen

Inhaltsverzeichnis

Starting Off: The Basic Parts of Speech – Die Wortarten

Meine Ziele

Nach Bearbeitung dieses Kapitels kann ich

- die verschiedenen Wortarten definieren und in ihrer ‚Funktion' unterscheiden;
- einige Beispiele für jede Wortart nennen.

1 Übersicht

English	Definition	German	Examples
noun	a person, animal or thing	**Hauptwort**	president, elephant, car
pronoun	stands for a person or thing	**Fürwort**	he, you, it, our, them, mine
article	stands before a noun	**Artikel**	the, a, an
adjective	describes a noun	**Eigenschaftswort**	old, good, beautiful, nice
preposition	a little word before a noun or pronoun indicating place or time	**Vorwort**	in, on, at, to, into, from
verb	something you do	**Zeitwort**	sing, eat, run, learn
adverb	describes a verb, an adjective or an adverb	**Umstandswort**	quickly, slowly, happily
present participle	'-*ing*'-form	**1. Mittelwort**	walking, singing
past participle	third form of a verb	**2. Mittelwort**	walked, sung

Your Turn: 'Basic Parts of Speech'

Write the following words in the matching columns.

drug ■ learn ■ president ■ destroy ■ entertain ■ global ■ job ■ harmful ■ language ■ clever ■ company ■ discuss ■ important ■ dynamic ■ water ■ extreme ■ body ■ reduce ■ educate ■ vomit ■ obese

Nouns	Adjectives	Verbs

Ziele erreicht?

Read the clues below and complete the crossword with the correct terms for the parts of speech described.

Across
3. a person, animal or thing
7. third form of a verb *(two words)*
8. stands for a person or thing

Down
1. *'-ing'*-form *(two words)*
2. describes a noun
4. describes a verb, an adjective or an adverb
5. stands before a noun
6. something you do
7. a little word before a noun or pronoun indicating place or time

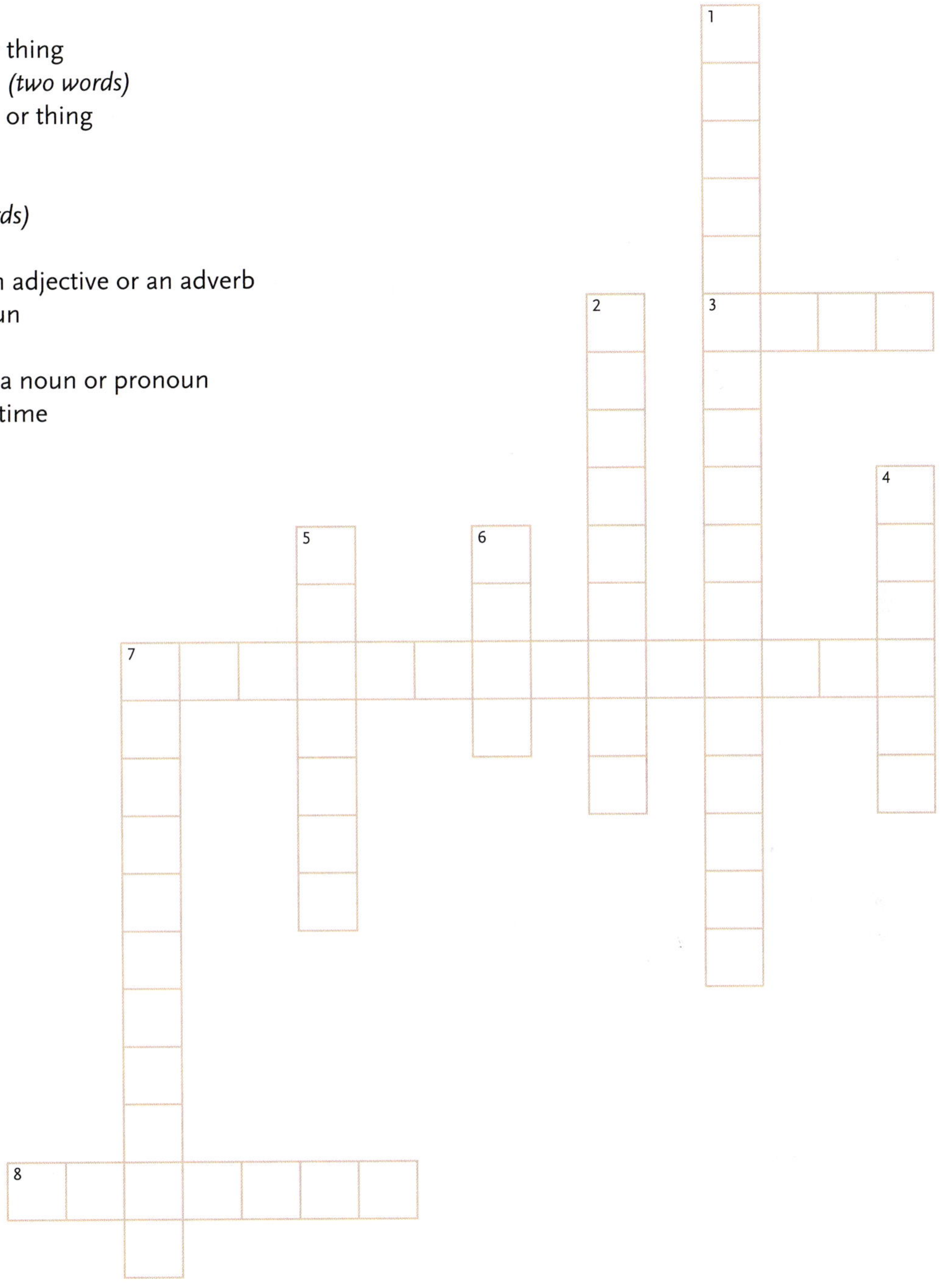

What did the lion say when he saw two hunters in a jeep?
Goodie – meals on wheels!

Adjectives and Adverbs – Eigenschafts- und Umstandswörter

Meine Ziele

Nach Bearbeitung dieses Kapitels kann ich

- mehrere Eigenschaftswörter vor einem Substantiv in der entsprechenden Reihenfolge anordnen;
- Umstandswörter richtig bilden;
- Eigenschafts- und Umstandswörter im Gebrauch unterscheiden;
- die Steigerungsformen korrekt bilden und dabei Besonderheiten berücksichtigen;
- die verschiedenen Möglichkeiten, Personen, Dinge etc. miteinander zu vergleichen, richtig anwenden.

1 The Adjective – Das Eigenschaftswort

1.1 Die Stellung

Das **Adjektiv** wird ausschließlich zur **näheren Beschreibung eines Substantivs** (= Hauptwort) verwendet. Werden mehrere Adjektive gleichzeitig verwendet, so ist stets die folgende Reihenfolge zu berücksichtigen.

Opinion	Dimension	Age	Shape	Colour	Origin	Material	Noun
interesting	big	old	round	red	British	plastic	book
boring	fat	young	square	blue	Austrian	brick	sweater
terrible	tall	new	oval	yellow	Canadian	concrete	gentleman
nice	short	modern	triangular	pink	Russian	wooden	woman
delicious	huge	ancient	rectangular	orange	Spanish	silk	town
	enormous			purple		paper	
	narrow						

huge = riesig **narrow** = schmal **ancient** = uralt **purple** = lila **brick** = aus Ziegel **concrete** = aus Beton

Im Englischen stellt man normalerweise **nie mehr als drei Eigenschaftswörter** vor ein Hauptwort.

Examples

- an **interesting new English** book
- a **small brown wooden** box
- a **nice little British** lady
- two **fat old furry** cats
- some **big yellow concrete** houses
- four **tall round** water tanks

Your Turn: 'The Adjective'

Your Turn 1

Place the adjectives in the correct order and combine them with the most suitable matching noun from the box below.

a blouse ■ a kitchen ■ a bed ■ a cap ■ socks ■ a text ■ a man ■ a peach

Model sentence

little | Spanish | nice: *a nice little Spanish lady*

1. English | long | boring: ______
2. pink | wooden | round: ______
3. red | delicious | big: ______
4. silk | new | green: ______
5. old | little | funny: ______
6. American | cotton | strange: ______
7. woollen | large | yellow: ______
8. white | new | beautiful: ______

1.2 Die Verwendung

1. Eigenschaftswörter **beschreiben Hauptwörter näher.**

Examples
- a **comfortable** chair
- a **nice** girl
- a **delicious** cake
- a **fast** car

2. Sie stehen in Sätzen mit einer **Form von *‚to be'*** und den **Sinnesverben** *(feel, taste, smell, sound, look)*, wenn sie das Subjekt am Satzanfang näher beschreiben.

Examples
- Tom **is** always **happy.**
- It **is perfect.**
- I **am** so **tired.**
- My teacher **is brilliant.**
- The new carpet **feels soft.**
- The cake **tastes delicious.**
- Fish **smells awful.**
- That **sounds great!**
- The blue dress **looks perfect.**

3. Sie werden weiters mit **Zustandsverben** *(become, get, grow, remain, turn)* und **Verben mit der Bedeutung ‚scheinen'** *(appear, seem)* verwendet.

Examples
- She **will become** a **famous** singer.
- It **was getting dark.**
- My soup **has grown cold.**
- He **remained silent** all the time.
- She **turned pale** when she saw him.
- She **appears** to be rather **upset.**
- It **seems hot** today.
- This task **seems** to be rather **difficult.**

4. Eigenschaftswörter können im Englischen – im Gegensatz zum Deutschen – nur eingeschränkt als Hauptwörter gebraucht werden.

a) Adjektive mit vorangestelltem ***‚the'*** bezeichnen eine **gesamte Personengruppe,** ebenso **Nationalitäten** auf *‚-sh'* und *‚-ch'*.

Examples
- the rich, the poor, the young, the old, the dead
- the Engli**sh**, the Fren**ch**, the Dut**ch**

b) **Einzelne Angehörige dieser Gruppen** werden durch das Hinzufügen von *(wo)man, person* oder *people* bezeichnet, während jene der Gruppe auf *‚-se'* auch für Einzelpersonen verwendet werden können.

Examples
- a poor (wo)man, several poor (wo)men, poor people; an English(wo)man, most Dutch(wo)men
- the Chinese – a Chinese; the Portuguese – a Portuguese; the Japanese – a Japanese

c) **Nationalitätsbezeichnungen** auf *‚-an'* und *‚-on'* bilden hingegen den Plural auf *‚-s'* und können im Genitiv mit *‚-s'* stehen, ebenso das Adjektiv *‚Greek'*.

Examples
the Austrians, the Russians, the Asians; the Americans' fear of terrorists; the Britons, the Saxons; the Greeks' idea of paying taxes

d) Dasselbe gilt für **politische und religiöse Gruppierungen.**

Examples
the Communists, the Conservatives, the Catholics, the Protestants

Your Turn: 'The Adjective'

Your Turn 2

Complete the following sentences by translating the German expressions in brackets.

1. Mother Teresa took care of ______ (die Armen) in India.
2. ______ (Die Konservativen) won the elections in Great Britain.
3. The state should always provide enough money for ______ (die Kranken und die Behinderten).
4. Nowadays ______ (die Schwarzen und die Weißen) in the United States have the same rights, but not the same opportunities.
5. ______ (Die Chinesen), ______ (die Russen) and ______ (die Brasilianer) all live in very large countries.
6. Norman Mailer wrote the famous novel ______ ('Die Nackten und die Toten').
7. There are a lot of ______ (Arme) in Austria, although it is the country with the highest number of ______ (Reiche).
8. Fortunately, most ______ (Katholiken und Protestanten) in Northern Ireland are getting along with each other quite well now.
9. Many ______ (Engländer) would never think of abolishing the monarchy, and neither would ______ (die Holländer).
10. Every society should take care of ______ (die Alten, die Kranken und die Benachteiligten).

die Benachteiligten = disadvantaged

Little Sue: *"My aunt has a new baby."*
Tommy: *"What was wrong with the old one?"*

2 The Adverb – Das Umstandswort

2.1 Die Bildung

1. Die meisten Adverbien werden durch Anhängen von ‚*-ly*' an das Adjektiv gebildet.

Examples
- sad – sad**ly**
- quiet – quiet**ly**
- beautiful – beautiful**ly**
- amazing – amazing**ly**
- brave – brave**ly**
- surprising – surprising**ly**

2. Adjektive auf ‚*-le*' nach Konsonanten wandeln direkt in ‚*-ly*' um.

Examples
- gent**le** – gent**ly**
- horrib**le** – horrib**ly**
- possib**le** – possib**ly**

3. Zweisilbige Adjektive auf ‚-*y*' wandeln in ‚-*ily*' um, während einsilbige gewöhnlich auf ‚-*yly*' bleiben.

Examples
- easy – eas**ily**
- happy – happ**ily**
- dry – dr**yly/drily**
- shy – sh**yly**

4. Einige wenige auf ‚-*e*' ersetzen ebenfalls durch ‚-*ly*'.

Examples
- due – du**ly**
- true – tru**ly**
- whole – whol**ly**

5. Adjektive auf ‚-*ic*' hängen ‚-*ally*' an.

Examples
- fantast**ic** – fantast**ically**
- systemat**ic** – systemat**ically**

6. Adjektive, die bereits auf ‚-*ly*' enden, bilden das Adverb mithilfe von ‚*in a … way*', ‚*in a … manner*' oder ‚*in a … fashion*'.

Examples
- **in a** friendly **way**
- **in a** lovely **manner**
- **in a** lively **fashion**

7. Unverändert bleiben als Adverbien *fast, long, straight* und *low*, ebenso *doubtless* und *extra*.

Examples
- Do not speak so **fast.**
- Summer never lasts **long** enough for me.
- Let's come **straight** to the point.
- The helicopter flew **low** over our heads.
- He would **doubtless** have caused an accident.
- This is an **extra** strong box.

8. Das Adverb von *good* ist als einziges unregelmäßig und hat die Form *well*.

Examples
- I do not know him so **well.**
- We have to prepare **well** for the exam.

2.2 Die Verwendung

Adverbien beschreiben **Tätigkeitsverben** (= Zeitwörter), **Eigenschaftswörter, Partizipien** oder **andere Adverbien** näher. Zustandsverben wie z. B. **to be, to seem, to remain, to look, to taste, to feel, to smell** etc. werden mit einem Adjektiv verwendet.

Examples
- He plays the piano **beautifully.**
- The conference was **badly** organised.
- We were **terribly** sorry.
- The meal was **surprisingly** well prepared.
- We could not go out because it was raining **heavily.**
- The rooms were **nicely** decorated.
- The beautiful black dress is **amazingly** cheap.
- They were **terribly poorly** dressed.

Your Turn: 'The Adverb'

Your Turn 1

Complete the following sentences with the correct adverb forms of the German words in brackets. Use the English words from the box below.

correct ■ extreme ■ good ■ heavy ■ incredible ■ remarkable ■ sad ■ serious ■ slow ■ surprising ■ terrible ■ total

1. He drove ________________ (langsam) along the street.
2. This silk blouse is ________________ (schrecklich) expensive.
3. We could not play tennis yesterday because it was raining ________________ (stark).
4. Why do you never take me ________________ (ernst)?
5. The exam was ________________ (überraschend) short.
6. Anita speaks German rather ________________ (gut) and she is fluent in English too.
7. The meeting last week was ________________ (außerordentlich) well organised.
8. She looked at him ________________ (traurig).
9. You have done all the exercises ________________ (richtig).
10. He answered my questions ________________ (bemerkenswert) quickly.
11. The room in the luxury hotel we had booked was ________________ (unglaublich) cheap.
12. We were ________________ (völlig) amazed when we saw her on stage for the first time.

How do Inuits dress? – As quickly as possible.

2.3 Besonderheiten

Einige Adjektive bilden **zwei Adverbien,** die eine **unterschiedliche Bedeutung** haben.

Adjective	Adverb 1	Adverb 2	Examples
deep	**deep** = tief	**deeply** = zutiefst	▪ They had to dig deep for water. ▪ She deeply regretted her mistake.
direct	**direct** = direkt	**directly** = sofort, bald	▪ This train goes direct to Leeds. ▪ He will be with us directly.
fair	**fair** = fair	**fairly** = ziemlich	▪ The guest team did not play fair. ▪ She speaks French fairly well.
free	**free** = frei, gratis	**freely** = zwanglos	▪ He managed to break free from his attacker. ▪ We got in for free. ▪ The celebrities behaved quite freely at the party.
hard	**hard** = hart, schwer	**hardly** = kaum	▪ He had worked hard all his life. ▪ He could hardly stand the heat.
high	**high** = hoch	**highly** = höchst	▪ Planes fly high up in the sky. ▪ Our new teacher is highly qualified.
just	**just** = geradezu	**justly** = zu Recht	▪ It is just amazing! ▪ You were justly punished by him.
late	**late** = spät	**lately** = in der letzten Zeit	▪ She arrived late. ▪ I have not seen you lately.
near	**near** = nahe	**nearly** = beinahe, fast	▪ Her body trembled when the dogs came near. ▪ They had nearly finished their homework.
pretty	**pretty** = ziemlich	**prettily** = hübsch	▪ You are a pretty good dancer. ▪ She was prettily dressed for her birthday party.
ready	**ready** = fertig	**readily** = bereitwillig	▪ Do you offer ready-made meals? ▪ We answered the policemen's questions readily.

Your Turn: 'The Adverb'

Your Turn 2

Adjective or Adverb? – Fill in the correct forms of the words in brackets.

1. He is a ______________________ (pretty, good) skier. He also skates ______________________ (fair, good).
2. These flowers smell ______________________ (nice). They will look ______________________ (perfect) on our dining table.
3. Jenny looks ______________________ (pretty) in her new dress. She knows how to dress ______________________ (pretty).
4. Susan is an ______________________ (excellent) cook. Her meals taste ______________________ (delicious). Every time she invites me for dinner I am ______________________ (ready) to eat anything she serves me.
5. Do not touch this material, it is ______________________ (high, explosive) and ______________________ (extreme, dangerous).
6. She felt ______________________ (deep) hurt by his ______________________ (rude) remark.
7. The teacher looked at me ______________________ (angry). He became ______________________ (pretty, furious) when I did not want to apologise for what I had done.
8. It had grown ______________________ (extreme, cold), and we felt ______________________ (desperate) and ______________________ (hopeless).
9. "Please, can you help me?" – "Just a moment, I'll be with you ______________________ (direct)".
10. She turned ______________________ (pale), after she had tasted the drink ______________________ (cautious). While I took her home ______________________ (quick), she remained ______________________ (silent) all the time.
11. At first this exercise sounded ______________________ (fair, difficult), but in the end it seems quite ______________________ (simple). I hope I did it ______________________ (perfect, good).
12. I hope this bus goes ______________________ (direct) to the Tower. My poor feet feel ______________________ (terrible).
13. Lizzy wants to become a ______________________ (famous) scientist. She is a ______________________ (high, gifted) girl, and she studies ______________________ (hard) every day. However, she ______________________ (hard) has time to see her friends.
14. Nowadays most elderly people have their pension transferred ______________________ (direct) to their bank account.
15. I cannot speak ______________________ (free). My husband is ______________________ (terrible, jealous), and he can get ______________________ (fair, aggressive).

cautious = vorsichtig

At work, John is giving a presentation on modern aeroplanes and finishes proudly: "Nowadays our planes can do anything a bird can do." From the back of the audience, someone shouts: "I'd like to see one of them lay an egg."

3 Comparison – Die Steigerung

3.1 Die Steigerungsformen

Adjektive und Adverbien werden im Englischen auf **zwei Arten** gesteigert.

1. Mithilfe der Endungen ‚*-er*' und ‚*-est*' steigern

einsilbige Adjektive.

Examples
- long – long**er** – long**est**
- fast – fast**er** – fast**est**
- cold – cold**er** – cold**est**
- hot – ho**tter** – ho**ttest**
- wet – we**tter** – we**ttest**

zweisilbige Adjektive auf ‚*-ow*', ‚*-y*', ‚*-le*' und solche, die auf der Endsilbe betont sind.

Examples
- narr**ow** – narr**ower** – narr**owest**
- easy – eas**ier** – eas**iest**
- noble – nob**ler** – nob**lest**
- polite – polit**er** – polit**est**
- severe – sever**er** – sever**est**

Wörter wie ***real*** oder ***wrong*** können im Alltagsenglisch nicht gesteigert werden!

2. Mit *more* and *most* steigern

alle übrigen zweisilbigen Adjektive.

Examples
- perfect – **more** perfect – **most** perfect
- distant – **more** distant – **most** distant

alle Adjektive auf ‚*-ing*' und ‚*-ed*'.

Examples
- interesting – **more** interesting – **most** interesting
- delighted – **more** delighted – **most** delighted

alle drei- und mehrsilbigen Adjektive.

Examples
- beautiful – **more** beautiful – **most** beautiful
- extraordinary – **more** extraordinary – **most** extraordinary

alle Adverbien auf ‚*-ly*'.

Example

carefully – **more** carefully – **most** carefully

3. Einige Formen werden unregelmäßig gesteigert:

Besondere Steigerungsformen
- good/well – better – best
- much/many – more – most
- bad/badly – worse – worst
- little – less – least

little = wenig

Doppelformen
- near
- old
- late
- far

near

near – nearer – nearest **(räumliche Entfernung)**

the nearest bus-stop = *die am nächsten gelegene Bushaltestelle*

near – nearer – next **(Reihenfolge)**
- the next patient = *der nächste Patient*
- the next stop = *der nächste Halt*

old

old – elder – eldest (vor oder statt eines Hauptwortes, besonders bei Familienmitgliedern)	***old – older – oldest*** (vor allem bei Vergleichen)
▪ my elder sister ▪ their eldest son ▪ the elder of the two ▪ the eldest in this family	▪ She is four years older than you. ▪ This is the oldest tree I have ever seen.

late

late – latter – last (Reihenfolge; als Gegensatz zu *former* oder *first*)	***late – later – latest*** (zeitliches Verhältnis; als Gegensatz zu *earlier*)
▪ her late partner ▪ the latter half of the 20th century ▪ the last thing I would do	▪ the latest news ▪ the latest fashion

far

far – farther – farthest (nur für räumliche Entfernung)	***far – further – furthest*** (für räumliche Entfernung und im übertragenen Sinn)
farther than a mile	▪ not further than a mile ▪ further details

⚠ ***Furthest* als Superlativ** ist generell üblicher als ***farthest:***
the furthest he has ever travelled (= das Weiteste, wohin er jemals gereist ist)

Your Turn: 'Comparison'

Your Turn 1

Choose the correct forms of the words in brackets.

injured = verletzt

1. The injured man was flown to the ______________ (nearest/next) hospital.
2. "What's the shortest way to the town-hall?" – "Take the ______________ (nearest/next) street on the left and then keep straight on."
3. At dinner I had to sit ______________ (nearest/next) to Uncle Jim.
4. Have you heard the ______________ (latest/last) news?
5. She always wears the ______________ (latest/last) fashion.
6. Our house is the ______________ (latest/last) one on the right side of the street.
7. Cricket and football are both English games, but the ______________ (later/latter) is more popular.
8. Innsbruck is ______________ (farther/further) away from Vienna than Graz or Linz.
9. If you would like to have ______________ (farther/further) information, please send me an email.
10. He is the ______________ (oldest/eldest) of the fifteen cousins I have. He is nine years ______________ (older/elder) than I am.

3.2 Der Vergleich

Es gibt vier verschiedene Möglichkeiten, Dinge miteinander zu vergleichen:

1. beide sind gleich

as … as

Example
My house is **as big as** your house.

2. beide sind nicht gleich

not as … as, not so … as

Examples
- Your car is **not as fast as** his car.
- Their kitchen is **not so modern as** yours.

3. eines ist größer, besser, schöner etc. als das andere

taller than …, better than …, more beautiful than …

Examples
- Our dog is **more beautiful than** yours.
- This new coat is **warmer than** the old one.

4. Eines ist weniger groß, gut, schön etc. als das andere

less big than, less good than, less beautiful than

Examples
- Mathematics is **less difficult than** English.
- Rabbits are **less clever than** dogs.

Die deutsche Steigerung mit **‚immer'** wird im Englischen durch **Verdoppelung** ausgedrückt.

Examples
- Every summer it gets **hotter and hotter.**
- **More and more** land is sold to Chinese companies.

Your Turn: 'Comparison'

Your Turn 2

Complete the sentences with the correct forms of the German expressions in brackets.

1. My Porsche is ______________ (schneller als) your Rolls Royce.
2. You are ______________ (dicker als) he is, you should eat ______________ (weniger).
3. Do you know Henning Mankell's ______________ (neuestes) book?
4. My cold is getting ______________ (immer schlimmer).
5. This house was ______________ (nicht so teuer). It cost ______________ (weniger als) yours.
6. My father is ______________ (älter als) my uncle, but he is ______________ (jünger als) my aunt.
7. Who made ______________ (die wenigsten) mistakes?
8. We must take him to the ______________ (das nächste) hospital.
9. We are prepared for the ______________ (das Schlimmste).
10. The hotel was ______________ (nicht so schön wie) in the catalogue.
11. The weather was getting ______________ (immer feuchter).
12. I find English ______________ (interessanter als) German. There are ______________ (immer mehr) people who speak this language.
13. Our cat is ______________ (schneller als) our dog. She is also ______________ (klüger).

⚠ Um größere und kleiner Unterschiede ausdrücken zu können, bedient man sich folgender Formen:

English	German	Examples
a little, a bit, slightly	ein wenig	The leather shoes were **a little/a bit/slightly** more expensive. They cost only two pounds more.
not quite, not nearly	nicht ganz so	Her mother is **not quite/not nearly** as nice as her father.
nearly, almost	beinahe	Spain is **nearly/almost** as large as France.
much, a lot, far	viel	Sweets are **much/a lot/far** better than fruit.

⚠ Bei **Superlativen** (= zweite Steigerungsstufe) kann man mittels **Ordnungszahlen** (*first, second, third, fourth, fifth* etc.) eine Reihung angeben und einen **deutlichen Abstand** durch ‚*by far*' ausdrücken.

Examples

- Tom is **the second best** football player in our school.
- Linz is **the third largest** city of Austria.
- Norway is **the fourth richest** country in the world.
- New Zealand is **by far the greenest** country I have ever been to.

Ziele erreicht?

Challenge 1 – Comparison

Compare the people, animals, places or items using the adjectives given in brackets. Look at the model sentence first.

Model sentence

Animals: mouse | cat | elephant | dinosaur (big)

A cat is much bigger than a mouse, but they are not nearly as big as an elephant.

An elephant is less big than a dinosaur. The dinosaur is the biggest animal.

1. Football players: Fernando Torres | Wayne Rooney | Cristiano Ronaldo | Lionel Messi (good)

2. Drinks: beer | wine | vodka | rum (strong)

3. Cars: Ford | Mercedes | Ferrari | Rolls Royce (expensive)

4. Animals: tortoise | dog | lion | cheetah (fast) — **tortoise** = die Landschildkröte **cheetah** = der Gepard

5. Austrian cities: Linz | Graz | Salzburg | Vienna (beautiful)

6. Family members: my mother | my father | my grandmother | my grandfather (old)

7. Bands: The Bee Gees | The Beach Boys | The Rolling Stones | The Beatles (successful)

8. Tourist countries: Sweden | Ireland | Spain | Italy (popular)

9. Actors: Brad Pitt | Johnny Depp | Will Smith | George Clooney (attractive)

10. The Simpsons: Lisa Simpson | Bart Simpson | Marge Simpson | Homer Simpson (tall)

Challenge 2 – Adjective or Adverb?

Fill in the correct forms of the words in brackets.

1. She emptied her drink ______ (quick) and said it tasted ______ (terrible).
2. I ______ (usual) go to work at seven in the morning. Today, however, I left later than ______ (usual).
3. His son died ______ (young). He died ______ (peaceful) at home.
4. She seemed to be rather ______ (irritated), for I heard her speaking ______ (angry) to her husband.
5. They tried to cross the lake. ______ (Lucky) the weather remained ______ (fine). They arrived just as it was getting ______ (dark).
6. Something went ______ (wrong), so they had to break the door open as ______ (quick) as possible.
7. The bridegroom looked ______ (handsome) in his new white suit; only his hair was not cut ______ (proper) and looked a little ______ (greasy).
8. I must tell you something about my new neighbour, but you must keep it ______ (secret).
9. If our president was ______ (wrong) informed, it would look ______ (bad) for the whole government.
10. As ______ (usual) the cat was sleeping ______ (quiet) in the kitchen. Her fur felt ______ (warm) and ______ (soft).
11. At first the children's story sounded ______ (strange) to us, but in the end it proved to be ______ (true).
12. "Does she feel ______ (happy) in her job?" – "Of course she does; she doesn't have to work very ______ (hard)."
13. This cake looks ______ (delicious), however it tastes ______ (awful).
14. It is ______ (terrible) ______ (hot) today. The fish will not keep ______ (fresh) for long in this weather. It does not smell ______ (good) anymore.

Challenge 3 – Comparison in Context

First, read the text. Then do the comprehension check below.

See 'Topics': Food and Trends

School Meal Take-up in England on the Rise

More than three million children in England have school lunches, including just over one million on free school meals, figures show. An extra 167,000 pupils took up the meals in 2011/12, compared with the year before. But not only the numbers, the price has also risen – a meal now costs £1.98 on average, compared with £1.93 a year ago.

Since 2008/09, almost half a million more children have switched from taking packed lunches to school to eating school dinners. In total, 46.3 % of England's primary school pupils and 39.8 % of secondary pupils had school dinners this year – the equivalent to 3.3 million pupils.

With more and more children eating school meals, it has become more important than ever to make sure the food they get tastes good, gives them the nutrition they need and that they have an experience which makes them want to go back for more. It is certainly encouraging to see that more and more children are opting for a school meal at lunchtime and are being served increasingly healthy and nutritious options. Everybody knows the benefits of a balanced meal on pupils' concentration and ability to learn.

Education Secretary Michael Gove announced an investigation of school dinners across the country and to establish an 'action plan' on how all schools can improve food standards. However, his plan was criticised by famous TV chef Jamie Oliver, who led a campaign seven years ago to improve school meals.

"We cannot afford to wait for the outcome of the Department for Education's latest assessment of food in schools. Knowing that one in three children is overweight or obese by the age of nine, we are obliged to act now. We owe this to our children, and we owe this to the future of our country."

KATHERINE SELLGREN – ADAPTED

Cross out the incorrect forms to make meaningful sentences.

1. **More than one million / less than half a million** children in England get free school meals.
2. Meals are **much cheaper / a bit more expensive** now than last year.
3. School dinners are becoming **as popular as / more popular than** packed lunches.
4. Nowadays it is **not so important anymore / more important than ever** that the food tastes good.
5. School meals **are healthier and more nutritious / less healthy and less nutritious** than before.
6. School dinners will be under **stricter / less careful** control than before.
7. JAMIE OLIVER is one of England's **most celebrated / most controversial** chefs.
8. He says that it **has become more urgent than ever / is not so urgent anymore** for the government to take effective measures in order to stop the trend of more and more children becoming overweight or obese.

What have hamburgers to do with outer space?
They are UFOs – Unidentified Frying Objects.

Challenge 4 – Adjective or Adverb in Context

Read the text and complete the sentences with the correct forms of the words in brackets.

See 'Topics': Ruining our Planet

London Looks to Tackle and Reduce its Mountain of Food Waste

In 2011 Boris Johnson, the then mayor of London, urged businesses and the public to sign an agreement to reduce the mountains of food __________________ (needless) thrown away and sent to landfill. The programme aims to make the capital a cleaner and greener city by cutting down food waste from __________________ (current) levels which are large enough to fill 11,720 double-decker buses a year.

At the 'Feeding the 5,000' event in Trafalgar Square, the Mayor called on businesses __________________ (simple) to follow a 'Food Waste Pyramid' guide to minimise how much __________________ (consumable) food is wasted. Firstly, by avoiding buying unneeded food, and secondly, by giving any __________________ (unwanted) food to charities such as FareShare and FoodCycle, which then give it to people in need. Thirdly, food __________________ (unfit) for human consumption should be fed to livestock where possible, and finally it should be disposed of __________________ (careful) by composting.

The Mayor handed out the first plate of __________________ (free) curry – made from vegetables which fail to meet the standards of supermarkets – at 'Feeding the 5,000', which aims to highlight the __________________ (enormous) quantities of __________________ (total) edible food that is disposed of every year. It is estimated that the average family wastes £ 50 each month by throwing away __________________ (unused) food still fit to eat.

The Mayor wants to reduce rubbish, create new green jobs and make London a cleaner and __________________ (environmental) friendlier city.

He has set out plans for managing London's waste, detailing that it would __________________ (easy) be possible to recycle 67 per cent of the waste created in London by using __________________ (renewable) technologies. This would reduce the impact of rubbish disposal on the environment __________________ (dramatical).

WWW.GREENWISEBUSINESS.CO.UK – ADAPTED

landfill = die Mülldeponie

to dispose of = entsorgen

"Dad, the boy next door said I look just like you."
"Really? And what did you answer?"
"Nothing, he was bigger than I."

Conditional Clauses – Die Bedingungssätze (‚*If*-Sätze')

Meine Ziele

Nach Bearbeitung dieses Kapitels kann ich

- die vier verschiedenen Grundformen der ‚*If*-Sätze' voneinander unterscheiden und erkennen;
- die passenden Verbformen bilden und in Bedingungssätzen anwenden;
- selbständig ‚*If*-Sätze' richtig bilden und verwenden.

1 Die Bildung und Verwendung

Die Bedingungssätze bestehen aus einem **Nebensatz,** der die **Bedingung** ausdrückt, und dem **Hauptsatz.**

Der Nebensatz kann durch die folgenden Konjunktionen eingeleitet werden:	
if	wenn, falls
unless	wenn nicht, falls nicht, außer wenn
in case	für den Fall, dass
on condition that	unter der Bedingung, dass
provided/providing (that)	vorausgesetzt, dass
supposing (that)	angenommen, dass
as long as	vorausgesetzt, dass

Nur wenn der **Bedingungssatz als erster** steht, wird er vom Hauptsatz durch ein **Komma** abgegrenzt.

Example
If he comes, I will tell him. → **ABER:** I will tell him if he comes.

Im Englischen gibt es **vier verschiedene Grundformen:**

'Type 0'

Für Bedingungen, die **immer wahr** sind und **erfüllt werden,** wie z. B. physikalische Tatsachen.

If-Satz	Hauptsatz
Present Tense	Present Tense

Examples
- If you **heat** water, at 212°F, it **boils** and **evaporates.**
- If you **strike** a match, it **starts** burning.
- If you **do not protect** your skin in summer, you **get** sunburnt.
- If I **am** late, my boss **gets** angry.
- If it **snows** in England, there **is** chaos on the roads.

to evaporate = verdampfen

Your Turn: 'Type 0'

Form meaningful sentences according to the model sentence using conditional clauses.

Model sentence
You travel in the sun for hours. You get sunburnt quite easily.
If you travel in the sun for hours, you get sunburnt quite easily.

1. You stop eating. You starve.

2. There is a lot of snow. Driving conditions are dangerous.

3. People eat too much junk food. They gain weight.
______
4. A serious hurricane hits Florida. The inhabitants leave the area.
______
5. I regularly watch the news in English. My English improves a lot.
______
6. Elderly people have a pet. They are happier.
______
7. We do a lot of sports. We are in good shape.
______
8. You grow up in China. You learn to speak Chinese.
______

'Type 1'

Für Bedingungen, die in der **Gegenwart oder Zukunft erfüllt werden (können).**

If-Satz	Hauptsatz
Present Tense	■ Future Tense ■ Modals ■ Imperative (für einen Befehl)

Examples

- He **will pass** his driving test if he **practises** more.
- If we **learn** Japanese, we **can/will be able to communicate** with people in Japan.
- **Get** ready if you **want to catch** the bus!

Your Turn: 'Type 1'

Your Turn 1

Fill in the correct forms of the words in brackets.

1. If I ______ (wake up) late on Monday, I ______ (miss) the bus.
2. If you ______ (move) to Cuba, you ______ (must speak) Spanish.
3. If you ______ (learn) hard, you ______ (pass) your maths exam.
4. If you ______ (eat) healthy food, you ______ (become) quite old.
5. If you ______ (not hurry up), you ______ (miss) your plane.
6. If you ______ (study) English three times a week, you ______ (improve) quickly.
7. If it ______ (rain) this weekend, we ______ (not go) on holiday to Hungary.
8. If you ______ (be) too busy, I ______ (not come) round for a cup of coffee.
9. If you ______ (not leave) my flat at once, I ______ (call) the police.
10. If she ______ (offer) me the job of personal assistant, I ______ (accept) this new opportunity.

Your Turn 2

Form meaningful sentences according to the model sentence. Use the expressions given in brackets.

Model sentence
I do not understand what you mean. (read our letter carefully)
If you read our letter carefully, you will understand what I mean.

1. You do not catch the next bus. (hurry up)
2. We cannot go to the lake. (finish early)
3. I do not help him. (ask me)
4. He cannot cut down the tree. (lend him your chain saw)
5. You do not arrive home in time. (drive faster)
6. She does not learn to play the piano. (practise more often)
7. We do not buy a bottle of red wine. (shops be open)
8. He need not put on his coat. (weather get colder)
9. Our boss cannot come to the meeting. (send him a taxi)
10. She does not understand. (teacher explains the rules again)

'Type 2'

Für Bedingungen, die eine **bloße Annahme** darstellen oder eine **Möglichkeit in der Zukunft** zum Ausdruck bringen.

If-Satz	Hauptsatz
Past Tense	Conditional I (*would* + Infinitive) Modals (*could, should, might* + Infinitive)

Examples
- If I **had** the money, I **would pay** my debts.
- Father **would be** angry if he **knew** what you are doing.
- If you **sent** her a message, she **would be** happy.
- It **would be** nice if we **went** to see Granny at the weekend.
- If we **had** our own boat, we **could go** on a sailing cruise in summer.
- She **should be** happy if he **sent** her a bunch of roses.
- If you **worked** overtime more often, your boss **might give** you a pay rise.

⚠ ***To be*** hat im ***If*-Satz** in der **Past Tense** immer die Form ***were.***

Examples
- If I **were** you, I would not go to that party.
- He'd offer you some help if he **were not** so busy.

Your Turn: 'Type 2'

Your Turn 1

Fill in the correct forms of the words in brackets.

1. If I ____________ (be) ten years younger, I ____________ (emigrate) to Australia.
2. We are always late! If we ____________ (leave) punctually at six o'clock, we ____________ (not have) any stress catching the early morning train.
3. If I ____________ (be) a politician, I ____________ (fight) for free health care and education.
4. If you ____________ (drink) too much alcohol, you ____________ (feel) sleepy quite easily.
5. If you ____________ (have) a spanner, you ____________ (can fix) your bike.
6. If we ____________ (have) more money, we ____________ (invest) most of it in schools.
7. If I ____________ (speak) Japanese fluently, I ____________ (travel) to Japan.
8. If I ____________ (be) slimmer, I ____________ (buy) designer clothes.
9. If I ____________ (have) more time and money, I ____________ (can stop) working and ____________ (go) abroad.
10. If I ____________ (be) you, I ____________ (buy) that new car.

spanner = der Schraubenschlüssel

Your Turn 2

Form conditional clauses according to the model sentence.

Model sentence
He does not have a car. He does not take you to the station. *If he had a car, he would take you to the station.*

1. I do not leave now. I do not catch the bus.
____
2. She does not have time. She does not come to the party.
____
3. I have to work. I cannot go on holiday this summer.
____
4. He does not love her. He does not want to marry her.
____
5. Mrs Adams does not exercise enough. She is not in good shape.
____
6. I am not a millionaire. I cannot go on a cruise around the world.
____
7. He is not a farmer. He does not have to get up early.
____
8. We go by train. We do not arrive early enough.
____
9. My mother is not a good cook. I never get a hot meal for lunch.
____
10. His parents do not go to the pub. They do not have many friends.
____

A doctor advised a very fat man to take up golf for exercise.
"That's no good to me," said the patient, "I've tried it before. If I put the ball where I can hit it, I can't see it, and if I put it where I can see it, I can't hit it!"

'Type 3'

Für Bedingungen, die eine **bloße Annahme** darstellen, weil sie **in der Vergangenheit nicht erfüllt** wurden.

If-Satz	Hauptsatz
Past Perfect Tense	Conditional II *(would have* + Past Participle)

Examples
- If we **had left** earlier, we **would have arrived** in time.
- I **would have helped** you if you **had asked** me earlier.
- You **would have succeeded** if you **had tried** harder.
- If he **had studied** medicine, he **would have become** a doctor.

⚠ Es können **Mischtypen** entstehen, wenn sich **beide Satzteile auf verschiedene Zeitstufen beziehen.** Der Hauptsatz drückt ein Resultat in der Gegenwart aus oder deutet auf einen Bezug zur Gegenwart hin z. B. durch Zeitangaben wie *now* oder *today*.

If-Satz	Hauptsatz
Past Perfect Tense	Conditional I *(would* + Infinitive)
Past Tense	Conditional II *(would have* + Past Participle)

Examples
- If you **had not been wearing** a warm coat, you **would** certainly **be** ill now.
- The children **would not do** that if they **had not been told** to.
- If it **had not been** so cold, the lake **would not be frozen** now.
- If he **were not such** a fool, he **would have told** the truth.

Your Turn: 'Type 3'

Your Turn 1

Fill in the correct forms of the words in brackets.

1. If I ____________ (be) interested in watching this film, I ____________ (go) to the cinema much sooner.
2. If you ____________ (spend) so much money on your new car, I ____________ (be) quite angry with you.
3. If she ____________ (invite) me to her birthday party earlier, I ____________ (go) there.
4. If you ____________ (take) the test last week, you ____________ (feel) more relaxed today.
5. My life ____________ (be) different if I ____________ (stay) in Paris five years ago.

6. If he ________ (wear) a suit, he ________ (get) this job yesterday.
7. If they ________ (not drink) so much alcohol, they ________ (not cause) that serious accident.
8. If the girl ________ (not be) so shy on the first day at her new school, she ________ (make) a lot of new friends.
9. If I ________ (buy) the tickets in advance, I ________ (go) to the concert last weekend.
10. If I ________ (not take) the wrong turning at King's Cross, I ________ (not arrive) late for the dance show. However, I was ten minutes late, so I missed the beginning.
11. If she ________ (not eat) so much at lunch, she ________ (can run) faster and ________ (catch) the bus.
12. They ________ (find) the house more easily if they ________ (have) a Sat Nav.

in advance = im Voraus

Your Turn 2

Form meaningful conditional clauses according to the model sentence. Some words need to be adapted.

Model sentence
They did not invite us, so we did not go to the party.
If they had invited us, we would have gone to the party.

1. We did not take an umbrella with us, so we got quite wet in the rain.
____
2. She was not careful enough, so she made a serious mistake.
____
3. It was terribly hot yesterday, so the farmers did not work in the fields.
____
4. The salary was rather poor, so she did not stay at the company.
____
5. You drank too much wine and vodka last night, so you have a hangover now.
____
6. My father wasted all his money gambling, so my parents could not buy a house of their own.
____
7. The Tigers did not play well, so they did not win the match.
____
8. He left the fridge door open in the morning, so he wasted a lot of energy.
____
9. Susan did not do her homework, so she got a bad mark.
____
10. Nobody told us about the nuclear accident, so we could not protect ourselves.
____
11. We did not find a cheap hotel room, so we had to spend our holidays at home.
____
12. Organic apples were too expensive. So I did not buy any at the market this morning.
____

Teacher: *"Now, Harrison, if your father borrows £ 10 from me and pays me back £ 1 a month, at the end of six months how much will he owe me?"*
Harrison: *"£ 10, Sir."*
Teacher: *"I'm afraid you don't know much about arithmetic, Harrison."*
Harrison: *"I'm afraid you don't know much about my father, Sir."*

Ziele erreicht?

Challenge 1 – Mixed Types

Fill in the missing forms of the verbs in brackets.

1. If I have the money, I ______ (buy) an electric car.
2. If I were you, I ______ (try) to stop eating so much junk food.
3. You ______ (can) talk to Jorge if you had learnt some Spanish.
4. Phosphorus ______ (burn) if you expose it to air.
5. If it ______ (stop) snowing, we will go skiing in the afternoon.
6. If the gunman ______ (come) through the garden, he would have left some footprints.
7. If the president were here, he ______ (tell) us what to do.
8. She probably would not have developed an eating disorder if her parents ______ (support) her more when she was a teenager.
9. If you had not bought this big old house, you ______ (not must pay) such high costs every month.
10. We ______ (need) another planet if we go on wasting resources like that.
11. If the government had not passed laws to cut down emissions, more than half of our woods ______ ______ (die) due to acid rain in the 1970s.
12. If the film 'The Sound of Music' were not watched all over the world, a lot fewer tourists ______ (come) to Austria every year.

Challenge 2 – Mixed Types: Situations

Finish the sentences in a meaningful way.

1. Do not do that. You will get into trouble if ______.
2. We cannot leave Grandpa alone anymore. If I had not dropped in at his flat this morning, ______ ______.
3. To be honest, your suit would look a lot better if ______.
4. I think he is only after her money. He would not have proposed to her if ______ ______.
5. He is not fit enough for the Olympics. If he trained harder, ______.
6. I had to do a lot of overtime this week. I would have learnt more if ______.
7. You must look after your garden better. The flowers will die if ______.
8. We had to stay at home all weekend. If it had not been raining, ______.
9. Tom refuses to share housework. If his wife had a full-time job, ______.
10. Global warming is a serious problem. If the polar ice caps melt, ______.

Indefinite Pronouns and Quantifiers – Die unbestimmten Für- und Zahlwörter

Meine Ziele

Nach Bearbeitung dieses Kapitels kann ich

- die verschiedenen unbestimmten Für- und Zahlwörter unterscheiden und korrekt verwenden;
- die Quantitätsbezeichnungen im Gebrauch voneinander unterscheiden und richtig anwenden;
- alle unbestimmten Für- und Zahlwörter im Kontext korrekt gebrauchen.

Unbestimmte Fürwörter sind unter anderem ***some, any, all, no, each*** und ***every.*** Zu den **unbestimmten Zahlwörtern** gehören die **Quantitätsbezeichnungen *much, many, a lot of, little*** und ***few.*** Sie können sowohl selbständig wie ein Substantiv als auch wie ein Adjektiv oder Adverb gebraucht werden. Die Verwendung im Detail ergibt sich aus den untenstehenden Vorgaben, die allerdings nur Richtlinien sein können.

1 Indefinite Pronouns – Die unbestimmten Fürwörter

1.1 *Some – Any*

Some und *any* bezeichnen eine unbestimmte Menge oder Anzahl im Sinn von ‚etwas', ‚einige'.

- ***Some*** und seine Zusammensetzungen *(= compounds)* stehen vorwiegend in bejahten Aussagesätzen und in höflichen Fragen.

***Some* wird vorwiegend verwendet:**

In der Bedeutung von ‚etwas' vor nicht zählbaren Substantiven im Singular

Examples
- Bring us **some** beer, please.
- Have **some** more tea, Susan.
- Cannot you give him **some** work? He seems to be bored.

Im Sinn von ‚einige' vor Pluralformen

Example
I would like to have **some** picture postcards, please.

Selbständig vor *of* oder in Bezug auf ein vorausgehendes Substantiv

Examples
- Would you like **some** of these biscuits?
- I borrowed **some** of your clothes.
- Did you take the oranges? – I took **some,** but not all. **Some** were good, **some** were bad.

In der Bedeutung von ‚irgendein' vor Singularformen

Examples
- **Some** man has asked to see you.
- They went to **some** place in India.
- I read it in **some** book.

Im Sinn von ‚ungefähr' vor Zahlenangaben

Examples
- There were **some** twenty people at the concert.
- He waited for **some** thirty minutes.

In höflichen Fragen

Examples
- Can you bring me **some** paper, please?
- Tom, would you like **some** cake?

In Zusammensetzungen wie *someone/somebody, something, somehow, sometime, somewhere, somewhat*

Examples
- There is **somebody** who wants to see Josie.
- Ask me **something** else.
- **Somehow** he always escapes.
- Last time we met **sometime** in June.
- It is **somewhere** near the station.
- She is **somewhat** difficult.

Customer: *"Waiter, bring me a cup of coffee without any milk, please."*
Waiter: *"We haven't got any milk, sir. What about some coffee without any cream?"*

- ***Any*** und seine *compounds* werden in der Regel in verneinten Sätzen, in Entscheidungsfragen und in Bedingungssätzen bei Ungewissheit oder Zweifel verwendet.

Any wird vorwiegend verwendet:

Im verneinten Satz, in der Frage, wenn die Antwort ungewiss ist und im Bedingungssatz nach *if/whether,* ebenfalls wenn Ungewissheit oder Zweifel besteht

Examples

- She does not want to have **any** more tea.
- Do you have **any** stamps?
- Did they meet **any** of their friends?
- I do not know if there is **any** more coffee in the pot.

⚠
- Didn't I give you **some** money this morning? I'm sure I did! *(= kein Zweifel)*
- If they had **some** money, they would buy the car. *(= positive Annahme)*

Vor allem im gesprochenen Englisch vor einem Substantiv, an Stelle von *a* oder *one*

Examples

- There is not **any** pharmacy in this village.
- Do you have **any** brother or sister?

Vor Komparativen (= 1. Steigerungsstufe)

Examples

- Does that feel **any** better?
- I do not want to stay **any** longer.

Im bejahten Satz im Sinne von ‚irgendein/ganz gleich welcher' und in den Wendungen *in any case/at any rate* (= auf jeden Fall, jedenfalls)

Examples

- You can come **any** day you like.
- **Any** help is better than no help!
- **At any rate,** he cannot be the thief.

Nach *without* und Adverbien wie *never, hardly, scarcely* oder *barely,* ebenso bei Verben, die eine Verneinung beinhalten wie z. B. *to refuse* (= ablehnen), *to deny* (= verweigern)

Examples

- He managed to carry the box without **any** help.
- They have hardly **any** money left.
- The hospital refused to accept **any** more patients.

In Zusammensetzungen wie *anybody/anyone, anything; anyhow, anyway, anywhere*

Examples

- Have you met **anybody?"**
- Is there **anything** new?
- It does not make sense **anyhow.**
- **Anyway,** we do not want to leave.
- Are you going **anywhere** tonight?

Your Turn: *'Some – Any'*

Fill in *some* or *any* or a **compound.**

compound = die Zusammensetzung

1. There is ________________ orange juice left in the carton.
2. Susan wanted to have ________________ more biscuits, but there were not ________________ left.
3. If there are ________________ problems, please discuss them with your group leader.
4. Is there ________________ here who speaks Spanish? There is ________________ at the door and I do not understand ________________ he is saying.
5. I would like to buy ________________ new clothes, but I do not have ________________ money left.
6. Do you have ________________ idea who that man was?
7. You can come and visit me ________________ time you want.
8. Are there ________________ letters for me?

9. Do not let ______________ in! I am too busy to see ______________!
10. I cannot see my keys ______________.
11. Mother did not think that Paul would pass his A-levels, but he managed ______________.
12. David looked so miserable yesterday. ______________ must have really upset him.

1.2 *Each – Every – All – Whole*

Each wird verwendet:

In der Bedeutung ‚jeder (einzelne)', alleine oder vor einem Substantiv

Examples
- She gave **each** child an apple. **Each** of them ate it at lunch.
- **Each** time I come in you are eating chocolate.

Im Sinne von ‚je' nach Zahlen

Examples
- She gave them two **each.** *(= Sie gab ihnen je zwei.)*
- The shirts cost seven pounds **each.** *(= Die Hemden kosten je sieben Pfund.)*

Every wird verwendet:

In der Bedeutung ‚jeder, alle' vor einem Substantiv, oft als Singularform zu *all*

Examples
- **Every** student had done their homework.
- **Every** time I see her we go for a coffee.
- **Every** day he takes the bus to work.

In der Verbindung mit Zahlen und einem Substantiv im Plural, vor Ordnungszahlen wie im Deutschen mit einem Substantiv im Singular

Examples
- **every** two days = **every** second day, **every** other day *(=jeden zweiten Tag)*
- on **every** other line *(= in jeder zweiten Zeile)*

In Zusammensetzungen wie *everyone/everybody, everything, everywhere*

Examples
- In our little village **everyone** knows **everyone** else.
- **Everything** went according to plan.
- She could see his friendly face **everywhere.**

All wird verwendet:

In der Bedeutung ‚alle', entweder selbständig oder vor einem Substantiv im Plural

Examples
all (the) boys, **all** men, **all** our friends, **all** the others

In der Bedeutung ‚ganz, alle(s)', entweder selbständig oder vor einem Substantiv im Singular

Examples
all I know, **all** day, **all** the time, **all** her money, **all** this

In der Bedeutung ‚ganz, völlig' als Adverb

Examples
- That is **all** wrong. *(= Das ist völlig falsch.)*
- That is **all** true, believe me!

In der Bedeutung ‚umso' vor Komparativen (= 1. Steigerungsstufe)

Example
If that is so, **all** the better. *(= Wenn das so ist, umso besser.)*

Whole **wird verwendet in der Bedeutung ‚ganz' im Sinne einer ungeteilten Ganzheit:**

Vor Substantiven	Selbständig
Examples the **whole** nation, the **whole** truth, a **whole** year, three **whole** days	**Examples** on the **whole** *(= im Ganzen)*, as a **whole** *(= als Ganzes)*; the **whole** of England *(= ganz England)*

Your Turn: *'Each – Every – All – Whole'*

Fill in ***each, every, all*** or ***whole.***

1. "Have you finished __________ the exercises?" – "Yes, I've already done __________ sentence."
2. Dad buys a bunch of flowers for Mum __________ other week.
3. My mother has three sports cars, and __________ of them run well.
4. Look, Tom has eaten the __________ apple pie. Only the crumbs are left!
5. He has four dogs. __________ of them have been trained.
6. __________ student must hand in the paper by tomorrow.
7. Yesterday __________ thing went wrong. The computer had broken down, and I had to write __________ letter by hand.
8. He kept ringing me up __________ afternoon to ask me if I would go out with him tonight.
9. __________ her cousins are rather tall, and __________ of them lives abroad.
10. I am starving. Can I have the __________ pizza, please?
11. __________ month his grandmother sent him __________ the money he needed.
12. __________ is well that ends well.

crumbs = die Brösel

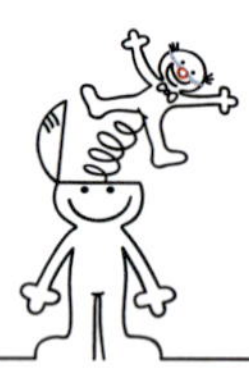

Teacher: *"Tom, you should have been in class an hour ago!"*
Tom: *"Why, did I miss anything good?"*

1.3 *Everybody – Somebody – Anybody – Nobody*

Nach den Zusammensetzungen ***everybody, somebody, anybody*** und ***nobody*** steht das **Verb** immer **im Singular.** Als zugehörige Pronomina werden die Pluralformen *their* und *themselves* verwendet.

Examples

- **Everybody** is invited.
- There is **somebody** in the garden.
- Is **anybody** at home?
- **Nobody** appears to be coming to the meeting.
- **Everybody** took **their** children to Disneyland.
- **Anyone** can become a member, can't **they?**
- She made the gesture of **somebody** cutting **their** throat.
- **Nobody** had put on **their** jackets.

Your Turn: *'Everybody – Somebody – Anybody – Nobody'*

Translate the following sentences.

1. Jeder muss sich die Hände waschen, bevor er sich zu Tisch setzt.
2. Er hatte keinem gesagt wohin er ging, daher wusste niemand wo er war.
3. Als das Feuer ausbrach, nahmen alle ihre Taschen und versuchten, die Notausgänge zu erreichen.
4. Alle behielten es für sich, was sie gerade dachten.
5. Jeder kann sich seine Lieblingsfarben aussuchen und anfangen, seinen Pullover zu stricken.
6. Niemand darf jetzt sein Haus betreten, es ist zu gefährlich.

Worried lady to pilot: *"You will bring me down safely, won't you?"*
Pilot: *"Don't worry, madam, I've never left anybody up here yet!"*

2 Quantifiers – Die unbestimmten Zahlwörter

2.1 *Much – Many – A Lot of*

1. ***Many*** wird verwendet für **zählbare Substantive,** die eine Pluralform bilden können. ***Much*** steht vor **Stoffnamen und unzählbaren Dingen,** die keine Pluralform haben, wie zum Beispiel *water, money, food* etc. Beide Formen stehen vorzugsweise in **verneinten Sätzen** und in **Fragen.**

   Examples
   - She has not got **many** friends.
   - Have you invited **many** people to his party?
   - I do not have **much** time this morning.
   - Does he earn **much** money?

2. Im **bejahten Satz** stehen ***much*** und ***many*** nur als **Subjekt mit *of*** und in Verbindung mit ***as, so, how*** und vorangestelltem ***too.***

   Examples
   - **Many of** us were ill last weekend.
   - **Much of** what he said was true.
   - You can eat and drink **as much as** you like.
   - There is one plate **too many.**
   - I don't know **how many** times I asked you to quit smoking.

3. Im **bejahten Satz** werden in allen anderen Fällen – vor allem im gesprochenen Englisch – Ausdrücke wie ***a lot of, lots of*** (colloquial), ***plenty of*** oder ***a great/good deal of*** bevorzugt.

   Examples
   - He has retired, so he has got **plenty of** time now.
   - We have **a lot of/lots of** friends.
   - The gallery showed **a great/good deal of** interest in his paintings.

2.2 *Little – Few*

Die Verwendung von *little* und *few*:

Few **wird verwendet in der Bedeutung ‚wenige' als Gegenteil zu *many;* es steht vor zählbaren Substantiven im Plural.**	***Little*** **wird verwendet in der Bedeutung ‚wenig' als Gegenteil zu *much;* es steht entweder allein oder vor einem unzählbaren Substantiv.**
Examples ■ He is a man of **few** words. ■ **Few** of my friends have children. ■ We had to wake her up every **few** hours. *(= alle paar Stunden)* ■ There were **fewer** people at the concert that expected.	**Examples** ■ The children see their father very **little.** ■ She has very **little** knowledge of literature. ■ The exercise was **less** difficult than I had thought.
⚠ *a few* = einige, ein paar	⚠ *a little* = ein wenig, ein bisschen
Examples ■ I will call you in **a few** days. ■ She has a lot of friends, but she only sees **a few** of them regularly. ■ There are **a few** things we must talk about.	**Example** ■ Can I have **a little** more, please? ■ He knows **a little** about everything.

Your Turn: *'Much – Many – A Lot of/Little – Few'*

Fill in the appropriate forms of quantifiers.

1. The fire was coming closer and closer, and there was not ________________ (viel) time left to leave the area.
2. The data on CO_2 emissions and global warming contain ________________ (viele) mistakes and inaccuracies.
3. Children whose parents are actors see very ________________ (wenig) of their parents in the evenings and at weekends.
4. There is not ________________ (viel) evidence that functional food keeps you fit and healthy.
5. In Austria ________________ (weniger) people will be affected by the rise of the sea level than in the Netherlands.
6. Nowadays, ________________ (immer weniger) families have three or ________________ (mehr) children.
7. Why did you not study ________________ (mehr) this year? I am ________________ (ein bisschen) disappointed by your marks.
8. My mother had ________________ (wenig) knowledge about healthy food and cooking, but she always spent ________________ (viel) time with me and my younger brother.
9. Slacklining is definitely not my kind of sport. It is ________________ (viel) more difficult than I had imagined.
10. I still need ________________ (ein paar) interesting books to take with me on holiday.
11. She is ________________ (ein bisschen) shy, and nobody asked her for a dance.
12. You cannot go swimming; there is not ________________ (viel) water in the pool.

evidence (Sg.) = die Beweise
functional food = die angereicherten Lebensmittel

Mother: *"Finish up your porridge so that you will grow up to be a pretty girl."*
Daughter: *"Why didn't you eat any porridge when you were little then?"*

Ziele erreicht?

Challenge 1

Translate the following sentences.

1. In seinem Wohnzimmer habe ich nicht viele Bücher gesehen. Es lagen einige Zeitungen auf dem Tisch, und in der Küche gab es ganz viele Kochbücher.
2. Dieses Hotel ist viel schöner als viele andere, die wir schon gesehen haben.
3. Du musst in den Supermarkt gehen, es ist nur mehr ein bisschen Brot da, und im Kühlschrank ist keine Milch mehr.
4. Ich bin ohne Gepäck nach England geflogen, es gibt so viele tolle Geschäfte dort, wo jeder etwas findet.
5. „Kann ich bitte noch etwas Obst haben?" – „Ich kann dir ein paar Kirschen und Erdbeeren anbieten."
6. „Er hat nur wenig Fortschritte gemacht, er muss mehr üben." – „Ja, er ist etwas faul."
7. Er isst sehr viel Junk Food. Zum Frühstück braucht er ein paar Burger und ganz viele Milchshakes.
8. Alle meine Freunde können Spanisch, jeder von ihnen möchte nach Südamerika reisen.
9. Nach seinem Unfall konnte er sich nur wenig bewegen. Er hat jeden Tag viel trainiert und alles getan, was er konnte. Jeder ist froh, dass es ihm wieder besser geht.
10. Jeder weiß, dass dein Vater nicht mehr viel arbeiten kann. Er kümmert sich aber sehr um seine Enkelkinder.
11. Es stimmt nicht, dass wir nichts gegen den Hunger auf der Welt tun können. Jeder kann etwas weniger Fleisch essen und ein bisschen Geld spenden.
12. „Machst du bitte auf, wenn jemand an die Tür klopft?" – „Ja, aber es wird keiner so bald in der Früh zu uns kommen."
13. „Kann ich bitte noch etwas Hühnchen haben?" – „Tut mir leid, es ist keines mehr da. Ich kann dir ein paar Würstchen in der Mikrowelle heiß machen."
14. In den europäischen Ländern rauchen weniger Leute, nachdem in den vergangenen Jahren das Rauchen an den meisten öffentlichen Orten verboten worden ist. Viele rauchen weniger, nur die Teenager rauchen mehr denn je.
15. Karen hatte niemandem erzählt, wo sie auf Urlaub war. Keiner wusste, wo sie war.
16. Frauen arbeiten noch immer viel mehr im Haushalt, bekommen aber weniger Geld als Männer und kaum Anerkennung für das, was sie tun.

A man stopped his car at a set of traffic lights in Dublin.
The lights kept changing: Red – Yellow – Green – Red ...
Finally a policeman came up to him and leant into the car.
"What's the matter, sir?" he asked. "Haven't we got any colours you like?"

Challenge 2

Fill in the appropriate forms of indefinite pronouns and quantifiers.

See 'Topics': Sports and Recreation

Sedentary Lifestyle Can Kill

The world is just days away from the greatest global showcase of elite sport. But while a ________________ thousand athletes will be pushing their bodies to the limit, ________________ of the world will be watching on TV, sitting inactive for hours on end.

The scientists say they are neither Olympics kill-joys nor are they advocating punishing gym sessions. As Pamela Das from the Lancet puts it: "It is not about running on a treadmill, whilst staring at a mirror and listening to your iPod. There's ________________ thing wrong with going to the gym of course, but the aim is to encourage ________________ one to build physical activity into their daily lives, such as by walking, cycling, swimming, gardening or doing ________________ sport they enjoy. The trouble is, ________________ that sounds familiar. We ________________ know we should move more and sit ________________."

Despite that, one in three adults worldwide fails to do the recommended 150 minutes of moderate aerobic physical activity per week. In the UK two out of three adults don't manage it. The Lancet scientists have opted to show the harm caused by inactivity. Around the world, they have found, lack of exercise is responsible for about as ________________ deaths a year as smoking, namely 5.3 million.

However, there are ________________ weaknesses in the data. The researchers have had to rely on the results of questionnaires sent out to 122 countries in which people self-report their levels of activity. Dr Lee, Harvard Medical School, says they were very cautious: "Our estimates of ill-health from lack of physical activity are, if ________________ thing, on the low side."

The outlook for the next generation seems bleak. A staggering four out of five 13–15 year olds globally do not do the recommended 60 minutes of activity ________________ day. The researchers say the problem of inactivity has reached pandemic levels, with far-reaching health, economic, environmental and social consequences. They call for a radical re-think in how to deal with the issue.

But rather than simply focusing on the bad, the benefits of being active have to be emphasised: ________________ thing that gets worse when we get older, gets better when we exercise.

Fergus Walsh, BBC News – adapted

to advocate = dafür sein

treadmill = das Laufband

lack of = der Mangel an

to rely on = sich verlassen auf

cautious = vorsichtig

bleak = trostlos

staggering = erschütternd

to emphasise = hervorheben

Infinitive and Gerund – Infinitiv und Gerundium

Meine Ziele

Nach Bearbeitung dieses Kapitels kann ich

- unterscheiden, wann man Infinitivkonstruktionen mit und ohne *to* verwendet;
- das Gerund richtig bilden und gebrauchen;
- Sätze mithilfe von Gerund- oder Infinitivkonstruktionen verkürzen oder sinnvoll miteinander verbinden;
- Infinitiv und Gerund im Kontext korrekt anwenden.

1 The Infinitive – Die Nennform

1.1 Der Infinitiv mit *to*

Er wird in der englischen Sprache so wie im Deutschen verwendet:

1. Nach **vielen Verben.**

Examples
- The teacher **tried to** contact the students.
- Do you **agree to** sign this contract?
- She **decided to** leave Canada.
- He **failed to** tell her the truth.
- The police-officer did not **hesitate** to shoot at the burglar.
- We **pretended to** be famous singers.
- A lot of children **refuse to** eat spinach.
- Would you **like to** go to the cinema tonight?

to pretend = vorgeben

2. Nach **bestimmten Verben + Objekt.**

Examples
- Mother **allowed me to** go to the party.
- He **advised her to** see a doctor.
- The wind **caused us to** go in.
- They **encourage him to** talk to her.
- We **expect you to** arrive on time.
- She **forced him to** buy her a ring.
- Susan **invited us to** have tea with her family.
- My father **taught me to** shoot.

to advice = anraten
to encourage = ermutigen

⚠ Nach ***wish*** und ***want*** folgt ebenfalls ein ***Objekt mit Infinitiv,*** im Unterschied zum Deutschen, wo ein Nebensatz mit ‚..., *dass*' steht.

Examples

German	English	Wrong
Wir möchten, dass du uns hilfst.	We **want you to** help us.	~~We want that you help us.~~
Tom möchte, dass wir um sieben dort sind.	Tom **wants us to** be there at seven.	~~Tom wants that we are there at seven.~~

3. Zur **Verkürzung eines Satzes,** wenn der Nebensatz das gleiche Subjekt hat.

Vor allem

nach Ordnungszahlen und Superlativen

Examples
- He was **the first to appear** and the last to go.
- During a hurricane **the best thing to do** is to stay in the basement.

anstelle eines indirekten Fragesatzes

Example
She did not know **whether to laugh** or **cry.**

mit bestimmten Ausdrücken

Examples
- She **was too tired to answer.**
- Is he really **such a fool as to believe** her?
- Would you be **so kind as to open** the door for me?

basement = das Untergeschoß

4. In der gesprochenen Sprache in Phrasen mit ***for*** + **Objekt** anstelle eines Nebensatzes.

for **+ Objekt**

it is hard, difficult, easy, common, wrong, impossible etc., oft mit *too* (vorangestellt) oder *enough* (nachgestellt)	*it is the custom, it is the rule, it is not uncommon, it is time* etc.

Examples

- It was **difficult for** her to live in a foreign country.
- It was **easy for** us to find him.
- It is still **common for** little girls to wear dresses.
- It is **wrong for** you to hit other children.
- It was **impossible for** him to do what he had always been dreaming of.
- It was **too hard for** her to give in.
- The box was **too heavy for** me to carry.
- The theatre was **near enough for** us to walk.
- The house is **big enough for** a family to live in.

Examples

- **It was time for** us to leave.
- Nowadays **it is not uncommon for** young people to live with their parents.

Your Turn: 'Infinitiv mit *to*'

Translate the following sentences using the correct infinitive forms.

1. Sie vereinbarten, sich am nächsten Tag um 8:00 im Konferenzraum zu treffen.
2. Bevor ich sechzehn war, ließen mich meine Eltern nie alleine fortgehen.
3. Das Beste was man für ein Kind tun kann ist es zu lieben und seine Bedürfnisse zu respektieren.
4. Er beschloss, seiner Frau nichts davon zu erzählen.
5. Unsere Lehrerin möchte, dass wir neue Vokabel am gleichen Tag lernen.
6. Dieses Büro ist zu klein für uns alle, um den ganzen Tag darin zu arbeiten.
7. Sie war die erste, die nach dem Mittagessen fragte und die letzte, die uns ihre Hilfe anbot.
8. Er zwang die Arbeiterinnen jeden Tag Überstunden zu machen.
9. Wir gaben vor, achtzehn zu sein und versuchten in die Bar hineinzukommen.
10. Ich war zu müde, um mich mit ihm zu unterhalten.
11. Es ist heutzutage nicht ungewöhnlich, dass Frauen jüngere Partner haben.
12. Die ganzen Taschen waren für die alte Frau zu schwer zu tragen.
13. Die Belegschaft erwartet von ihrem Chef, dass er sie rechtzeitig informiert.
14. Würden Sie bitte so nett sein und das Fenster zumachen?
15. Der Preis ist hoch genug, dass die Bauern das ganze Jahr von ihrem Gewinn leben können.
16. Die Kinder luden uns ein, mit ihnen zu singen und zu feiern.

1.2 Der Infinitiv ohne *to*

Er wird verwendet

nach den Hilfsverben *can, may, must, shall, will* und *need.*

Examples
- There is something you **can do** for me.
- **May** I **ask** you a favour?
- You **must** never **do** that again.
- He **will be** back soon.

nach bestimmten Redewendungen wie z. B. *would rather/sooner* (würde lieber) und *had better* (Es wäre besser, wenn ...).

Examples
- I would **rather leave** than stay here.
- She would **sooner die** than ask for help.
- You **had better do** what your parents say.

mit Verben der Sinneswahrnehmung + Objekt.

- ***feel*** (fühlen)
- ***hear*** (hören
- ***watch*** (beobachten)
- ***notice*** (bemerken)
- ***see*** (sehen)

Examples
- He **felt the lion come** closer and closer.
- We **heard her smash** the window and escape.
- She **noticed him cross** the street.
- I **saw you enter** the house last night.
- They **watched him buy** fruits and vegetables.

in Phrasen in der Bedeutung ‚jemanden etwas machen lassen'.

- ***let*** [(zu)lassen]
- ***make*** (zwingen)
- ***have*** (veranlassen)
- ***not have*** (nicht zulassen)

Examples
- He always **let** her **do** it her way.
- The teacher **made** us **do** our homework again.
- He **had** the secretary **type** the letter.
- I will **not have** him criticise my work.

⚠ Im **Passiv** wird bei ***make*** der Infinitiv mit ***to*** verwendet.

Examples
- We **were made to** get up very early.
- The girl **was made to** clean the floor every evening.

Your Turn: 'Infinitiv mit oder ohne *to*'

Translate the following sentences using infinitive forms with or without ***to.***

1. Unsere Mutter lässt uns unter der Woche viel Zeit mit unseren Freunden verbringen.
2. Sein Lehrer ermutigte ihn dazu, Schriftsteller zu werden.
3. Es ist Ärzten erlaubt, ihre Patienten gratis zu behandeln.
4. Dein Auge sieht nicht gut aus, du solltest lieber einen Arzt aufsuchen.
5. Der Polizist ließ mich 30 Euro Strafe zahlen, weil ich zu schnell gefahren war.
6. Der Bürgermeister befahl uns ins Rathaus zu kommen.
7. Meine Oma ließ mich einmal in der Woche meine Schuhe putzen.
8. Ihre Eltern erlaubten ihr, bei ihrer Freundin zu übernachten.
9. Paul gab mir den Ratschlag, für ein Jahr ins Ausland zu gehen.
10. Ein strenger Lehrer lässt die Schüler alle Sätze auswendig lernen.
11. Sie sahen wie der Dieb die Geldbörse aus ihrer Handtasche stahl.

12. Der Doktor erlaubte dem Patienten nicht, noch länger zu rauchen.
13. Wir können nicht zulassen, dass er diese Drogen nimmt.
14. Die Regierung unterstützte die Obdachlosen dabei, Arbeit zu finden.
15. Meine Mutter erlaubte uns nie Brot wegzuwerfen.
16. Er ließ seine Sekretärin den ganzen Bericht noch einmal tippen.

2 The Gerund – Das Gerundium

2.1 Die Bildung

Das Gerund wird gebildet aus dem **Infinitiv des Verbs und *‚-ing'*** und ist die hauptwörtlich gebrauchte Form des Verbs (= Verbalsubstantiv). Es bildet keinen Plural, kann aber u. a. einen **Artikel,** einen **Genitiv** oder **Adjektive** vor sich haben.

Examples
- Who does **the cleaning** this week?
- **John's singing** has got better.
- For this task **careful listening** is required.

2.2 Die Verwendung

Das Gerund muss verwendet werden

1. nach **bestimmten Verben** wie z. B.:

English	German
to admit	zugeben
to avoid	vermeiden
to consider	erwägen, überlegen
to delay, to postpone	auf-, verschieben
to deny	leugnen
to enjoy	gerne tun
to finish	aufhören

English	German
to imagine, to fancy	sich (etwas) vorstellen
to mind	sich etwas daraus machen
to miss	versäumen
to practise	üben
to risk	riskieren
to suggest	vorschlagen

Wenn man sich nicht sicher ist, ob ein Verb das Gerund oder den Infinitiv verlangt, kann man dies mithilfe des Wörterbuchs herausfinden.

Examples
- He **admitted being** the thief.
- She always **avoids looking** at me.
- We are **considering leaving** Austria.
- They **delayed opening** the new building.
- He **denies stealing** the money.
- My partner **enjoys playing** football.
- Have you **finished doing** your homework?
- I **imagined living** in Italy.
- Would you **mind sitting** down?
- She **missed handing** in the paper on time.
- I **practised jumping** from the wall.
- He **risked losing** all his money.
- We **suggested going** on a skiing holiday.

2. in Verbindung mit den Verben ***go*** und ***come.***

Examples
- We have to **go shopping** today.
- They **went dancing** together.
- He cannot **come sailing** with us.

3. nach ***need*** und ***want*** an Stelle des Infinitivs im Passiv in der Bedeutung ‚es nötig haben, müssen, es brauchen'.

Examples
- My hair **wants cutting** (= wants to be cut) regularly.
- This matter **needs explaining** (= needs to be explained).

4. nach einer **Präposition** in Konstruktionen wie z. B.:

English	German
to apologise for	sich entschuldigen für
to believe in	glauben an
to congratulate somebody on	jemandem gratulieren zu
to depend on	abhängig sein von
to dream of	träumen von
to insist on	bestehen auf
to keep somebody from	jemanden abhalten von
to look forward to	sich freuen auf
to punish somebody for	jemanden betrafen wegen/für
to prevent somebody from	jemanden abhalten von
to rely on	sich verlassen auf
to speak/talk about	sprechen/reden von/über
to succeed in	gelingen zu

English	German
to take an interest in	Interesse daran haben zu
to have experience of	Erfahrung haben mit
to be on the point of	im Begriff sein zu
to be used to	es gewöhnt sein zu
to be famous for	berühmt sein wegen
to be fed up with	es satt haben zu
to be good at	gut sein beim
to be fond of	etwas gerne machen
to be interested in	interessiert sein an
to be proud of	stolz sein auf
to be tired of	es satt haben zu
to be afraid of	Angst haben zu

Examples
- The teacher **insisted on correcting** the students' texts.
- Are you **fond of eating** out with friends?
- The manager **has succeeded in solving** this difficult problem.
- Many pupils believe they **are** not **good at writing** compositions.
- The client has **apologised for** not **calling** our office earlier.
- We should **prevent** teenagers **from taking** up smoking.

5. nach **Phrasen** wie z. B.:

English	German
to be busy	damit beschäftigt sein zu
to be worth	wert sein ... zu werden
what about	wie wäre es, wenn

English	German
cannot help	nicht anders können als zu
feel like	Lust haben; nach ... zumute sein
cannot stand	es nicht ertragen zu

Examples
- When she entered the office he **was busy talking** to a customer.
- This novel **is** really **worth reading.**
- **What about going** to the disco tonight?
- It was so funny that she **could not help laughing.**
- I **cannot stand sitting** in a coffee shop for hours.

Your Turn: 'Gerund'

Translate the following sentences using gerund forms.

1. Wir konnten sie nicht davon abhalten, ihn zu heiraten.
2. Mein Vater bestand darauf, dass wir nach Italien auf Urlaub fahren.
3. Susan ist berühmt dafür, dass sie köstliche kleine Kuchen bäckt.
4. Gestern gelang es mir zum ersten Mal, den Baum hinaufzuklettern.
5. In der Volksschule war er damit beschäftigt Lesen und Schreiben zu lernen.
6. Er war schon immer daran interessiert, neue Leute kennenzulernen.
7. Ich habe es satt, dass du immer zu spät kommst!
8. Er war gerade dabei wegzugehen, als seine Freunde kamen.

6. Zur Satzverkürzung mit Präpositionen wie ***after, before, in, on, by, instead of, without, for, because of*** etc., wenn beide Satzteile das gleiche Subjekt haben.

Examples

After they had spent some time with us they went home.	→	After spending some time with us they went home.
When he was leaving the house he bumped into his mother-in-law.	→	On leaving the house he bumped into his mother-in-law.
She did not stay in bed, she went to work.	→	Instead of staying in bed she went to work.
When they left, they did not say good-bye.	→	They left without saying good-bye.

Your Turn: 'Satzverkürzungen mit Gerund'

Connect each sentence pair with a preposition and a gerund construction.

1. We swam in the warm lake. Then we had a picnic.
2. She did not go on holiday. She stayed at home all summer.
3. They entered the hall. However, they did not greet us.
4. I left the supermarket late at night. I bumped into an old friend.
5. He was sentenced to sixteen years in prison. He had killed his wife brutally.
6. We went to the cinema. First we had to finish our work.
7. They did not help him. They ran away.
8. We were crossing the street. We saw his car driving along the river.

A postman walked into a hospital complaining that a dog had just bitten him on the leg.
"Did you put anything on it?" asked the doctor.
"No," answered the postman. "He liked it just as it was."

3 Gerund or Infinitive – Gerundium oder Nennform

Es gibt einige Verben, die sowohl mit Gerund als auch mit dem Infinitiv stehen können:

start, begin, continue, intend

Sie können mit Gerund oder Infinitve stehen, ohne dass es einen Bedeutungsunterschied gibt.

Examples

- It **started to rain.** = It **started raining.** *(= Es fing an zu regnen.)*
- We **began to read.** = We **began reading.** *(= Wir begannen zu lesen.)*
- They did not **intend to stay** longer. = They did not **intend staying** longer. *(= Sie hatten nicht vor länger zu bleiben.)*

like, dislike, love, hate

**Das Gerund bezieht sich auf eine allgemeine Aussage,
während der Infinitiv entweder eine Gewohnheit oder einen bestimmten Einzelfall ausdrückt.**

Examples

- I **love playing** golf, but I do not **like to play** when it is too hot.
- She **hates cleaning,** and she especially hates **to clean up** other people's mess.
- He **likes to take** the bus to Charing Cross at 7.15.

⚠ **ABER:** In Verbindung mit ***would*** steht **immer der Infinitiv.**

Examples

- I **would like to meet** your brothers and sisters at the weekend.
- He said he **would hate to have** to report me to the police.

stop, remember, forget, regret

Das Gerund verweist auf die Vergangenheit.

Examples

He **stopped smoking** a few weeks ago.
(= Er hat vor ein paar Wochen aufgehört zu rauchen.)

She will never **forget kissing** him.
(= Sie vergisst nie wie er sie geküsst hat.)

We will always **remember being** with you.
(= Wir erinnern uns immer daran, wie wir bei euch waren.)

I deeply **regret saying** that to you.
(= Ich bedaure zutiefst, dass ich das zu dir gesagt habe.)

Der Infinitiv bezieht sich auf eine nachfolgende, zukünftige Handlung.

Examples

I **stopped to talk** him about the weather.
(= Ich blieb stehen, um mit ihm über das Wetter zu reden.)

Don't **forget to buy** some bread for supper!
(= Vergiss nicht Brot für das Abendessen zu kaufen!)

You must **remember to switch** off the computer.
(= Du musst daran denken den Computer auszuschalten.)

I **regret to tell** you that you did not get the job.
(= Es tut mir leid Ihnen mitteilen zu müssen, dass Sie die Stelle nicht bekommen haben.)

try

mit Gerund = ‚etwas ausprobieren, etwas versuchsweise probieren'	mit Infinitiv = ‚(mit Anstrengung) versuchen, etwas zu tun'
Examples He **tried speaking** Spanish to them, but they did not understand what he wanted. *(= Er kann ein bisschen Spanisch, er hat es versucht, aber sie haben ihn leider nicht verstanden.)* If you cannot relax, **try doing** yoga regularly. *(= Probier es doch mal mit Yoga, vielleicht klappt es!)*	**Examples** He **tried to remove** the tree from the road so that they could go on travelling. *(= Er hat alle seine Kräfte aufgeboten, um die Straße freizubekommen.)* We **tried to convince** her not to leave. *(= Wir haben alles versucht, um sie umzustimmen.)*

Your Turn: 'Gerund or Infinitive'

Fill in the correct forms of the verbs in brackets.

1. We must stop ________________ (pollute) the oceans and start ________________ (protect) our environment.
2. Most parents would like their children ________________ (study) medicine or law.
3. She regrets ________________ (spend) such a lot of money on clothes and shoes.
4. You must not forget ________________ (order) new carpets and curtains for the guest rooms.
5. He tried ________________ (get up), but he was too weak.
6. My mother loves ________________ (buy) organic fruit and vegetables at the weekly market.
7. Tom hated ________________ (wait) for his wife, as he was in a hurry as usual.
8. Instead of ________________ (go) on a diet, try ________________ (exercise) more.

Teacher: *"Why did the Stone Age man draw pictures of hippopotamuses and rhinoceroses on cave walls?"*
Stephen: *"It's probably because he was fed up with spelling them."*

Ziele erreicht?

Challenge 1

Fill in the correct forms of the verbs in brackets.

1. She is really looking forward to ________________ (have) another baby.
2. Would you remember ________________ (invite) your parents for the weekend?
3. He offered to ________________ (help) me carry one of my suitcases.
4. I am used to ________________ (work) in my office till late at night.
5. We tried ________________ (speak) to him, but he was not available all day.
6. You should save your money for something else – the film is not worth ________________ (watch).
7. She insisted on his ________________ (hand over) the car keys, because he had already had three pints of beer.

8. I am afraid you did not remember ______ (call) our boss this morning.
9. He suggested ______ (go) to the hotel bar to have another drink.
10. Stop worrying! Simply try ______ (do) it!
11. We generally like ______ (climb) mountains. However, as it is raining today, we would prefer ______ (stay) at home.
12. Can you imagine ______ (be) a celebrity like MADONNA or DAVID GUETTA?
13. We would really love ______ (go) to America this summer, however, we did not remember ______ (apply) for a visa.
14. You promised ______ (not call) him. I must insist on your ______ (give) me your mobile.
15. He enjoys ______ (travel) a lot, and he wants me ______ (go) with him next time.
16. She could not help ______ (cry). It was such a moving film.
17. What about ______ (have) a nice cup of tea and some scones?
18. He is not used to ______ (prepare) his lunch himself.
19. Have you ever tried ______ (cross) Lake Atter?
20. We succeeded in ______ (convince) our customers to buy our new computer.

Challenge 2 – If Women Ruled the World

Fill in the correct forms of the verbs in brackets.

See 'Topics': Men and Women

In her book former White House press secretary Dee Dee Myers explains why everything would change if women were in charge. ______ (empower) women would make the world a better place, because women are more cooperative and progressive than men, and they prefer ______ (have) a long conversation to ______ (shout) at each other.

Throughout history, women were proud of ______ (be) able to support men in leading positions.

Nowadays girls can aim ______ (be) school teachers or university presidents, doctors, engineers, entrepreneurs, or astronauts.

Before she started ______ (write) her book, she talked to friends, and she succeeded in ______ (interview) prominent and successful women, such as biologist Jane Goodall, Senator Dianne Feinstein, British activist and entrepreneur Anita Roddick and environmental activist Wangari Maathai.

Mrs Myers says: "This book is not supposed ______ (be) an attack on men. I think men have done wonderful things. But that doesn't mean the world wouldn't ______ (be) better if more women ______ (try) to take part in public life. If women were allowed ______ (have) more power, not just in the United States, but around the globe. If more women started ______ (get) access to education, economic resources and health care. If women had equal rights and equal opportunities. If more women were used to ______ (work) in boardrooms, classrooms, operating rooms and courtrooms. If men stopped ______ (give) women's ideas and opinions and life experiences less weight than their own. If people around the globe always remembered ______ (value) girls as much as boys. If women ruled the world."

Modal Auxiliary Verbs – Die modalen Hilfsverben

Meine Ziele

Nach Bearbeitung dieses Kapitels kann ich

- die verschiedenen Formen der Hilfsverben bilden;
- die Hilfsverben in allen Zeiten richtig abwandeln;
- die Umschreibungsformen im Kontext adäquat anwenden.

1 Die Bildung

1. Zu den ‚Modal Auxiliary Verbs' gehören ***can, may, must, shall, will*** und ***ought to.*** Sie sind ‚unvollständig' und werden daher wie die Hilfsverben im Deutschen gemeinsam mit dem Infinitiv (ohne to) des Hauptverbs verwendet. Die Verben ***need*** und ***used to*** können ebenfalls wie Hilfsverben verwendet werden.

Examples
- They **can** play football in the garden.
- We **must** see our dentist in the afternoon.
- I **should** go to the bank later.
- He **ought to** go to the dentist.
- You **need not** wash your clothes every other day.
- At primary school we **used to** wear uniforms.

2. Sie haben **kein ‚-s'** in der 3. Person Singular und bilden **kein Present Participle (*‚-ing'*) oder Past Participle (*‚-ed'*).**

Examples
- We **must go** to church now.
- You **cannot come** in at the moment.

3. Die **Frage** und die **Verneinung** werden immer **ohne *do*** oder ***does*** bzw. ***did*** gebildet.

Examples
- **Must** he really exercise regularly?
- **May** I have another cup of tea, please?
- I **could not** talk to him yesterday.
- They **will not** be on time.

⚠ Die Verneinung ***must not*** bedeutet ‚nicht dürfen'. Für ‚nicht müssen' wird die Form ***need not*** verwendet.

Examples
- Students **must not** cheat. = *Schüler/innen **dürfen nicht** schummeln.*
- We **need not** go to work today. = *Wir **müssen** heute **nicht** in die Arbeit gehen.*

4. Die meisten Modalverben haben eine Form der Present und der Past Simple: ***can – could; may – might; shall – should; will – would; need – needed.***

⚠ ***Must*** und ***ought to*** gibt es nur in der Present Tense Simple, wobei in der gesprochenen Sprache die Präsensform auch anstatt der Future Tense verwendet wird. ***used to*** bildet nur die Form der Past Tense Simple.

Examples
- I **must see** you tomorrow.
- You **can buy** new things next week.
- I **used to travel** a lot when I was young.

5. **Alle fehlenden Formen** sowie der **Infinitiv mit *to*** müssen durch **‚Ersatzformen'** ausgedrückt werden.

Modal Verb	Ersatzform	Examples
can	to be able to to manage to	When he was a child he **was not able to** climb a tree.
may	to be allowed to to be permitted to	The children **have been allowed to** play computer games for two hours now.
must	to have to/to be obliged to	We always **have to** wear protective gloves in the lab.
must not	not to be allowed not to be permitted to	She will **not be allowed** to go to the party next weekend.
shall	to be to	You **are to** wait here until I come back.
(will)	to want to/to wish to	They have always **wanted to** go and see him personally.

⚠ ***Will*** muss auch im Präsens ersetzt werden, da es die Future Tense bildet.

Examples

Present Tense	He **wants to** marry her. = *Er will sie heiraten.*
Future Tense	He **will** marry her. = *Er wird sie heiraten.*

6. Eine **Beziehung zur Vergangenheit** wird durch den **Infinitiv Perfekt *(have* + Past Participle)** hergestellt.

Examples
- He **could have done** better. = *Er hätte es besser machen können.*
- You **must have called** someone else. = *Sie müssen jemand anderen angerufen haben.*
- They **might have missed** the train. = *Sie werden wohl den Zug versäumt haben.*
- He **should have bought** a new car. = *Er hätte ein neues Auto kaufen sollen.*

Your Turn: 'Forms'

Put the auxiliaries **in bold** in the correct tense form in brackets.

1. I **can** swim across the lake. (Past Tense)

2. The prisoners **cannot** escape so easily. (Past Perfect Tense)

3. Pam **may** go out till midnight. (Present Perfect Tense)

4. We **must** plant a lot of trees in our garden. (Future Tense)

5. They **may** travel to Australia alone. (Past Tense)

6. You **cannot** buy this car. (Future Tense)

7. She **must** stay in this terrible place. (Past Perfect Tense)

8. Tourists **must** do a lot of sightseeing. (Present Perfect Tense)

9. The children **may** visit Disneyland with their parents. (Future Tense)

10. In Ireland a lot of people **must** live on potatoes. (Past Tense)

11. Greece **cannot** pay back its debts. (Present Perfect Tense)

12. Dogs **may not** enter this park. (Past Perfect Tense)

2 Die Verwendung

2.1 *Can*

1. ***To be able to*** bezeichnet im Gegensatz zu *can/could* eine **Fähigkeit in konkreten Einzelfällen** im Sinne von ‚in der Lage sein'.

Examples
- After some time he **was able to** free himself.
- We are so glad you **were able to** come!

2. Für eine **Erlaubnis** sind die Formen ***can/could*** in der Umgangssprache üblicher als may.

Examples
- **Can** I come in?
- He **could** go out whenever he liked.

3. Außerdem können die Formen ***can/could*** eine **Möglichkeit** oder in der **Verneinung ein Verbot** ausdrücken.

Examples
- You **cannot** do that!
- You **cannot** smoke here.
- The weather is fine, so I **can** mow the lawn.

4. Die verneinten Formen ***cannot/could not*** werden auch im Sinn von ***it is impossible that*** verwendet.

Examples
- My brother **cannot** be at home now; he has just called me from his office.
- He **cannot** have eaten all the cake, it was far too big!

2.2 *May/Might*

May/Might bezeichnet neben einer Erlaubnis auch eine Vermutung (deutsch: ‚kann vielleicht' oder ‚möglicherweise').

Examples
- You **may** be right!
- They **may** be sitting in the café now.
- That **might** be rather difficult.

2.3 *Must*

1. Im Vergleich zu ***must,*** das die **persönliche Meinung** ausdrückt, steht ***have to*** für **Verbote von außen** z. B. einer anderen Person oder Gesetzen.

Examples
- I **must** exercise regularly to keep fit.
- My doctor says I **have to** exercise regularly.
- In Britain pupils **have to** wear school uniforms.

2. ***Must*** drückt im Vergleich zu ***have to*** eine stärkere Verpflichtung aus, während ***ought to*** einer Empfehlung gleichkommt, die ihrerseits stärker als ***should*** ist.

Examples

- You **must** tidy up your room.
- You **have to** get up earlier if you want to be in time.
- You **should** buy this dress, it really suits you!
- You **ought to** tell your parents immediately.

3. ***Must not*** (= nicht dürfen) bedeutet immer ein **strenges Verbot,** die verneinte Form **‚nicht müssen'** wird durch ***need not*** ersetzt.

Examples

- She knows that she **must not** do that.
- We **need not** wear evening clothes on this occasion.

4. ***Ought to*** gibt es nur in der **Present Tense Simple.** Es kann meist anstelle von *should* verwendet werden.

Example

You still look rather pale. You **ought to** stay in bed until you get better.

Your Turn: 'Mixed Forms'

Fill in a suitable form of the modal verbs in brackets.

1. Although I was very tired last night, I ______ (must) finish my latest project.
2. Last week I invited some friends to dinner, but my best friend ______ (not can) come.
3. On Saturday I ______ (must) walk to the city centre, as public transport was not working.
4. He ______ (may) take the train instead of the bus.
5. Tom ______ (can) play the violin very well by the time he was eight.
6. These young children ______ (must) exercise more in their next summer holidays.
7. Yesterday I ______ (not can) find my car keys. I had to take a taxi.
8. The plane ______ (must land) by now.
9. My parents ______ (may spend) this weekend in Milan.
10. "Somebody has just called." – "That ______ (must) be my grandfather. He always calls me at five o'clock."
11. The neighbours called the police, so the students ______ (must) turn the music down.
12. My father ______ (cannot) accept the job offer because he did not want to move to South America.
13. Luckily I ______ (not must) work yesterday.
14. I do not think you ______ (shall) tell this story to the police.

2.4 *Used to*

Used to wird verwendet als Ausdruck einer **Gewohnheit in der Vergangenheit.**

Examples
- My grandma **used to** walk to the market.
- She **used to** travel by bus.
- She **used to** wear her best clothes to church.

Die Vergangenheitsform *used to* ist nicht zu verwechseln mit ***to be used to doing something*** (= gewohnt sein etwas zu tun), die in allen Zeiten verwendet werden kann.

Examples
- My little brother **is not used to walking long distances**.
- We **are used to having dinner** at six o'clock.

Your Turn: 'Modal Auxiliary Verbs'

Cross out the incorrect forms to make meaningful sentences.

1. When I was a child, I **used to go / am used to going** swimming in the lake.
2. I **used to speak / am used to speaking** in front of an audience. I am a teacher.
3. As a father I **used to clean up / am used to cleaning up** the mess my children make every evening.
4. When I was in the army I **used to get up / am used to getting up** at six every morning.
5. My grandmother **used to walk / is used to walking** five miles when she went to church on Sundays.
6. In the past, the football team 'Anderlecht' **used to attract / is used to attracting** the best Belgian players. Nowadays they cannot afford them.
7. I **used to read / am used to reading** the paper after lunch. That is one of the things I really enjoy.
8. In Spain you will soon **used to take / be used to taking** a siesta in the afternoon.
9. On our last holiday in Finland my wife **used to have / is used to having** a sauna every day.
10. After all this time I have become quite **used to operate / used to operating** this new programme.

Patient: *"Doctor, doctor, I keep thinking I'm a dog."*
Doctor: *"Sit down, please."*
Patient: *"Oh no – I'm not allowed on the furniture!"*

Ziele erreicht?

Challenge 1

Fill in the missing forms of the modal verbs given in German.

1. Mr Brown broke his leg last week. So he ______ (nicht können) go out for seven days.
2. In parks dogs ______ (müssen) be kept on a lead.
3. Even experts ______ (können) make mistakes.
4. When Joe was younger, he ______ (können) swim pretty fast.
5. Son: "______ (dürfen) I go to the disco tonight?"
   Father: "No, you ______ (nicht dürfen)."
   Son: "But Sue ______ (dürfen) go last week!"
   Father: "You ______ (dürfen) go when you are as old as Sue."
6. Mr Brown ______ (nicht können) help us tomorrow. He is ill. That is why we ______ (müssen) work alone.
7. You ______ (nicht brauchen) phone her, because she is not at home at the moment.
8. You ______ (müssen) do as I say.
9. Pat ______ (nicht, müssen) be at home before midnight.
10. Children ______ (eigentlich nicht sollen) eat many sweets.
    Instead, they ______ (sollen) eat more fruit.
11. Pat ______ (können) play the piano. He ______ (können) play the piano for five years.
12. There ______ (müssen) be a mistake.
13. The students ______ (müssen) work very hard for their A-levels next year.
14. We ______ (müssen) be quiet. Otherwise, we ______ (können) wake up the baby, and then mother will be angry.
15. Mr Smith missed the train. He ______ (nicht können) go to Vienna at seven and ______ (müssen) wait for the nine o'clock train instead.
16. Alice got top marks in her A-levels. So she ______ (müssen) be very clever.
17. She ______ (können) swim the English Channel soon.
18. They ______ (nicht brauchen) clean everything before they started to paint.

Bill: *"I can't make up my mind whether to be a poet or a painter."*
Monica: *"Oh, I think you should be a poet."*
Bill: *"You mean you've read one of my poems?"*
Monica: *"No, I've seen one of your paintings."*

Challenge 2 – Life in the German Democratic Republic

Read the text, then do the exercise below.

See 'Topics': Power to the people

In 1949, the German Democratic Republic was created out of the Soviet Zone of occupied Germany. It lasted until 1990 when the people voted to join the Federal Republic after the Berlin Wall had fallen the year before.

One of its greatest achievements was the creation of a society without class and gender privilege that offered educational and career prospect to everybody. Everyone had a right to education, a job and a roof over their head. Those who did heavy manual work, such as miners or steel workers, enjoyed certain privileges, like better wages and health care, than those in less exhausting or dangerous professions such as office work or teaching. No worker was sacked, unless for serious misconduct or incompetence. However, even in such cases, other alternative work would be offered.

achievement = die Leistung
career prospect = die Karriereaussicht

wage = der Lohn
exhausting = anstrengend
misconduct = das unkorrekte Verhalten

There were workplace clinics, doctors and dentists attached to large factories and institutions. Full-time childcare from the beginning helped to solve working parents' problems of caring for their children in the afternoons and during school holidays. The other side of the coin was that there was also a social obligation to work, and the GDR had no system of unemployment benefit because the concept of unemployment did not exist.

unemployment benefit = das Arbeitslosengeld

The economy of central planning enabled the government to plan growth, set priorities and determine where to invest. Due to its large scale, however, it was often inefficient and inflexible so that a lot of goods were not always available in the shops as they were in Western shops. Unlimited shopping was only possible in particular stores, and only with foreign money, such as West German Marks or US Dollars.

available = erhältlich

A lot of Western governments boycotted the GDR and introduced bans as a sign of protest. They did not agree with the political system of the GDR and the way it was treating its citizens. The government did not hold elections or allow the people to take part in any decisions. It left a lot to be desired concerning individual rights and democracy.

citizen = der/die (Staats)Bürger/in

The official security service, called 'STASI', kept people under surveillance if they criticised the system or any of its representatives. Friends, neighbours, even relatives and spouses were recruited to spy on and report one another to the police. People were imprisoned for such reasons as trying to leave the country, or telling political jokes. Prisoners were kept isolated and disoriented, knowing nothing of what was going on in the outside world.

to keep under surveillance = überwachen
to recruit = anwerben

Many could not cope with the restrictions und the subtle psychological terror and tried to leave the country, which was illegal without an exit visa. Between 1961, when the Wall was built, and the fall of the Berlin Wall hundreds tried to escape and leave the country secretly. Many of them were executed or sent to prison for life. Some well-known celebrities, such as writer and singer Wolf Biermann, were officially expatriated and expelled from the GDR.

subtle = spitzfindig

to expatriate = ausbürgern
to expel = ausweisen

Now describe some benefits and downsides of life in the former GDR. Form sentences using appropriate modal verbs.

Start like this:

- Everybody was able to …
- People were not allowed to …
- If they wanted to travel abroad, they had to …

Nouns and Articles – Die Hauptwörter und ihre Artikel

Meine Ziele

Nach Bearbeitung dieses Kapitels kann ich

- alle Hauptwörter richtig in die Mehrzahl setzen;
- Besonderheiten bei der Pluralbildung erkennen und die Verben entsprechend übereinstimmen;
- die Formen des Genitiv korrekt bilden und anwenden;
- bestimmte und unbestimmte Artikel richtig setzen;
- Hauptwörter und ihre Artikel im Kontext adäquat verwenden.

1 Singular and Plural Forms – Die Ein- und Mehrzahlformen

1.1 Die Bildung

1. Der Plural wird durch Anfügen der Endung ***‚-s'*** an das Wort im Singular gebildet. Nach Zischlauten wie [s/z/sch] wird ***‚-es'*** [iz] angehängt.

Examples

- girl – girl**s**
- boy – boy**s**
- bus – bus**es**
- box – box**es**
- wish – wish**es**

2. Endet ein Hauptwort auf **Konsonant und *‚-y'*,** ändert die Pluralform auf ***‚-ies'*.**

Examples

- ba**by** – ba**bies**
- la**dy** – la**dies**
- stor**y** – stor**ies**

3. In ein **paar Wörtern** auf ***‚-o'*** wird die Pluralform zu ***‚-oes'*.**

Examples

- potat**o** – potat**oes**
- tomat**o** – tomat**oes**
- (▪ negr**o** – negr**oes)**

⚠ Beachten Sie, dass das Wort *negroes* im täglichen Sprachgebrauch nicht mehr verwendet werden darf (‚politically incorrect').

4. In manchen Wörtern auf ***‚-f'*** oder ***‚-fe'*** wird der Plural mit ***‚-ves'*** gebildet, bei anderen mit ***‚-fs'*** oder ***‚-fes'*.**

Examples

- thie**f** – thie**ves**
- kni**fe** – kni**ves**
- wol**f** – wol**ves**
- roo**f** – roo**fs**
- sa**fe** – sa**fes**

5. Es gibt im Englischen **neun Hauptwörter,** die eine **eigene Pluralform** bilden. Diese sollten Sie sich merken.

- man – men
- woman – women
- child – children
- goose – geese
- ox – oxen
- mouse – mice
- foot – feet
- tooth – teeth
- louse – lice

Entsprechend werden auch zusammengesetzte Wörter in den Plural gesetzt.

Examples

- Englishman – Englishmen
- Scotswoman – Scotswomen

6. Manche Wörter wie ***sheep*** und ***fish*** haben im **Plural die gleiche Form wie im Singular,** ebenso einzelne Fischarten.

Examples

- sheep – sheep
- fish – fish
- trout – trout
- salmon – salmon
- tuna – tuna
- squid – squid

trout = die Forelle
salmon = der Lachs

squid = der Tintenfisch

Your Turn: 'Singular and Plural – Bildung'

Put the following words into the plural and read them out to a partner.

Singular	Plural	Singular	Plural
cherry		house	
potato		lady	
holiday		life	
woman		family	
pony		wish	
mouse		roof	
Scotsman		fox	
goose		fly	
story		half	
tomato		child	
radio		chief	
leaf		country	

1.2 Besonderheiten in der Verwendung

1. Zahlen wie ***million, thousand, hundred*** oder ***dozen*** stehen im **Singular,** wenn ein **Zahlwort** davor steht.

Examples
- three **thousand** years
- two **dozen** eggs
- five **million** pounds
- nine **hundred** cars
- five **hundred** thousand cows

2. Sie stehen im **Plural,** wenn **kein Zahlwort** vorangeht und die **Präposition *of*** folgt.

Examples
- thousand**s of** years
- dozen**s of** bottles
- million**s of** dollars
- hundred**s of** animals

3. **Maße, Gewichte und Währungen** haben nach Zahlwörtern im Plural die Pluralform.

Examples
- She weighs over 160 **pounds.**
- He is only five **feet** tall.

4. Wenn eine weitere Zahl nachfolgt oder wenn sie gemeinsam mit einem Zahlwort ein Eigenschaftswort bilden, haben Bezeichnungen wie ***foot*** oder ***pound*** die **Singularform.**

Examples
- eight **pound** ten
- six **foot** four
- a five-**pound** note
- a nine-**year**-old boy
- a ten-**foot** ladder

5. Im Britischen Englisch ist die Form ***people*** die **Pluralform von *a person.*** In der Bedeutung ‚das Volk' bildet es die Pluralform ***the peoples*** (= die Völker).

Examples
- At Christmas there are a lot of **people** in the street.
- **The peoples** of Asia still need to be united.

6. Bezeichnungen für **Kleidungsstücke und Körperteile stehen im Plural,** wenn sie sich auf **mehrere Personen** beziehen. Dies gilt auch für die Wörter ***life*** und ***mind.***

Examples
- The gentle**men** kept their **hats** on.
- The lad**ies** shook their **heads.**
- The **children** raised their **hands.**
- **They** have already made up their **minds.**
- **We** risked our **lives** to save the little girl.

Your Turn: 'Singular and Plural – Übereinstimmung'

Translate the following sentences using appropriate singular and plural forms.

1. Wir möchten gerne den Mantel anbehalten.
2. Die Leute sagen, die Chinesen sind ein fleißiges Volk.
3. Die Bank hat vierzig Millionen Dollar verloren.
4. Manche Leute haben sich dutzende Male den Film ‚Titanic' angesehen.
5. Es waren sechshundert Passagiere an Bord des Schiffes.
6. Tausende von Arbeitern bei GM sind im Streik.
7. Männer nehmen im Allgemeinen den Hut ab, wenn sie jemanden grüßen.
8. Unsere Freunde haben dutzende von Wein- und Bierflaschen eingekauft.
9. Es waren über zwanzig Personen in dem Kurs.
10. Das neue Einkaufszentrum kostete 10 Millionen Pfund.
11. Sie entschlossen sich, den Lehrer zu ignorieren und drehten ihm den Rücken zu.
12. Die Australier, Neuseeländer, Kanadier und Südafrikaner sprechen alle dieselbe Sprache.
13. Der Bankräuber hat fast zwei Millionen Pfund mitgenommen.

7. Manche **Hauptwörter** stehen in der **Singularform,** haben aber die **Bedeutung für den Plural.** Sie stehen immer **ohne den unbestimmten Artikel.**

Examples

advice	der Rat/die Ratschläge	**information**	die Information(en)
progress	der Fortschritt	**news**	die Nachricht(en)
knowledge	die Kenntnis(se)	**underwear**	die Unterwäsche
furniture	das Mobiliar, die Möbelstücke		

AUSNAHME: Eine Ausnahme der Regel bildet hier die Wendung ***a good knowledge of something.***

Example
My brother has **a good knowledge of English.** He is practically a native speaker.

→ Um diese Hauptwörter auch in der **Einzahl** verwenden zu können, muss ihnen ***a piece of*** bzw. ***some/a few/two pieces of*** vorangestellt werden.

Examples
- This is **an** interesting **piece of news.**
- My brother has bought **some** new **pieces of furniture.**

8. **Kleidungsstücke und Werkzeuge,** die aus **zwei gleichen Teilen bestehen,** gibt es **nur im Plural,** und zwar auch mit der **Bedeutung für den Singular.**

Examples

trousers	die Hose	**underpants**	die Herrenunterhose
jeans	die Jeans	**briefs**	der Damenslip
shorts	die kurze Hose	**spectacles/glasses**	die Brille
pyjamas	der Pyjama	**scissors**	die Schere

→ Um sie auch im **Plural** verwenden zu können, muss ihnen ***a pair of*** bzw. ***some/a few/two pairs of*** vorangestellt werden.

Examples

- She buys **four pairs of scissors.**
- I need **a pair of shorts** and **a pair of jeans.**

9. **Einige Wörter** werden **ausschließlich im Plural** gebraucht.

Examples

belongings	die Habe, der Besitz	**stairs**	die Treppe, die Stiege
clothes	die Kleidung	**surroundings**	die Umgebung
contents	der Inhalt	**thanks**	der Dank
goods	die Ware(n)	**wages**	der Lohn

10. **Das Verb muss mit dem Subjekt immer übereingestimmt werden.** Ist dieses Hauptwort im Singular, so stehen das Verb und ‚Begleiter' des Hauptwortes im Singular. Umgekehrt gilt dasselbe, wenn das Subjekt im Plural steht.

Examples

- **My grandmother's furniture is** very old.
- **This advice is** quite valuable for me.
- **Your scissors are** not sharp any more.
- **Our wages are** far too low.

AUSNAHME: ***The United States, The United Nations*** und Wörter auf ***‚-ics'*** gehen **immer** mit dem **Verb im Singular.**

Examples

- **The USA has** elected a new president.
- **Mathematics is** not her favourite subject.

Your Turn: 'Singular and Plural – Ausnahmen'

Translate the following sentences using appropriate singular and plural forms.

1. Hast du meine Schere gesehen? Sie ist nicht in der Lade.
2. Deine weiße Hose ist schmutzig, wir müssen sie waschen.
3. Hier sind die sieben Uhr Nachrichten.
4. Die Umgebung war ja ganz nett, aber die Möbel im Hotelzimmer waren alt und hässlich.
5. Das sind gute Neuigkeiten; wir bekommen heuer mehr Lohn als letztes Jahr.
6. „Wo ist mein Pyjama?" – „Setz deine Brille auf, er liegt auf deinem Bett!"
7. Die USA sind noch immer eine Weltmacht.
8. Vielen Dank für deine guten Ratschläge!
9. Geben Sie den Inhalt dieser Packung in eine Schüssel.
10. Physik ist ein wichtiges Fach, aber ich mag es gar nicht.
11. Die Damenbekleidung ist im ersten, die Herrenbekleidung im zweiten Stock.
12. Ich glaube, ich habe schon ganz gute Kenntnisse in Englisch.

Patient: *"Doctor, my family think I am mad."*
Doctor: *"Why?"*
Patient: *"Because I like sausages."*
Doctor: *"Nonsense, I like sausages too."*
Patient: *"You do? You must come round and see my collection. I have hundreds."*

2 The 'Saxon Genitive' – Der zweite Fall

2.1 Die Bildung

1. Im **Singular** wird der **Genitiv** durch das Anhängen von **,-'s'**, im **Plural** durch Anhängen von **,-s'"** gebildet.

Examples
- my father**'s** job, my mother**'s** room
- her sister**s'** dresses, our parent**s'** house

2. Die **unregelmäßigen Pluralformen** hängen wie im **Singular ,-'s'** an.

Examples
- the children**'s** toys
- the geese**'s** feathers

3. Bei **Eigennamen auf ,-s'** kann man entweder **,-'s'** oder nur ein Apostroph **'** anhängen. Die Aussprache bei ,-s' lautet [iz].

Examples
- Charles**'(s)** car [tʃa:lziz]
- James**'(s)** books [dʃeimziz]

Your Turn: 'Saxon Genitive – Bildung'

Use the correct genitive forms.

my sister – bike	my sister's bike	Mrs Pim – flowers	
the children – room		women – rights	
a woman – dress		our parents – boat	
the soldiers – guns		the child – desk	
Shakespeare – plays		the workers – wages	
my uncle – car		these men – hats	
her father – gift		Obama – speech	
our teachers – pens		the citizens – duties	
ladies – rooms		gentleman – hat	

2.2 Die Verwendung

1. Der ‚Saxon Genitive' gibt **die Besitzerin/den Besitzer einer Sache oder den/die Verursacher/in einer Handlung** an, vor allem bei **Personen und Tieren.**

Examples
- **Susan's** handbag
- **Tom's** wedding
- **Charles's** book
- **the dog's** kennel
- **the cat's** tail

Weiters wird der ‚Saxon Genitive' verwendet

bei Zeitangaben (oft auch Genitiv oder Adjektiv möglich)

Examples
- yesterday**'s** newspaper
- three hour**s'** drive (also: a drive of three hours/ a three-hour drive)

für ein Geschäft, ein Haus, eine Wohnung oder ein Gebäude

Examples
- the butcher**'s**
- the grocer**'s**
- at my aunt**'s**
- at my grandmother**'s**
- St Paul**'s**
- St Stephen**'s**

2. Bei **Dingen** steht dagegen der **Genitiv mit *of*.**

Examples
- **the tyres of** the car
- **the sails of** a ship

Der Genitiv mit *of* wird auch verwendet

bei Mengenangaben wie *cup, bottle, glass, pair, piece, kilo* etc.

Examples
- a **cup** of coffee
- a bottle of wine
- a kilo of ham

bei geographischen Bezeichnungen wie *state, town, city, isle, university* und nach *month, title, name, sort* und *kind*

Examples
- the **Isle** of Man
- the **City** of London
- the **University** of Illinois
- the **month** of December
- all **sorts** of people

⚠ Bei ***mount, lake*** und ***river*** **entfällt die Präposition *of*,** wenn der Name folgt. Ebenso verhält es sich mit **Jahreszahlen.**

Examples
- Mount Everest
- Lake Michigan
- the river Thames
- the year 1998

"Waiter, there's no chicken in this chicken pie."
"Well, sir, you don't get dog in a dog biscuit."

Your Turn: 'Saxon Genitive – Verwendung'

Translate the following sentences.

1. Die Rede des Chefs war viel zu lang.
2. Kennst du den Autor dieses Romans?
3. Geh bitte zum Bäcker und kaufe fünf Semmeln und ein Viertel Kilo Butter.
4. Wo ist die heutige Zeitung?
5. Wir sind heute bei meiner Oma eingeladen.
6. Nach einer einstündigen Rast gingen wir weiter.
7. Im Jahr 2009 verbrachten wir unseren Urlaub am Eriesee.
8. Ich kann die Frau meines Nachbarn nicht leiden.
9. Alle Fenster des Hauses waren offen.
10. Das Boot von Herrn Burns ist sehr schnell.
11. Ich hätte gerne ein Dutzend Eier und ein Pfund Speck.
12. Der Monat April ist oft kalt und regnerisch.
13. Der Fluss Amazonas ist der längste auf der Welt.
14. Die Stadt Wien ist berühmt für ihre schönen Gebäude und Museen.
15. Präsident Obama war einst Student auf der Universität Harvard.
16. Nach einem dreimonatigen Aufenthalt in London kam sie im Monat März nach Hause.
17. Kann ich bitte eine Flasche Bier oder ein Glas Wein haben? Ein Stück Käse wäre auch nett.
18. Sir Edmund Hilary war der erste Mensch auf dem Mount Everest.

Did you hear about the group of city boys who were out for a walk in the country? They came across a pile of empty milk bottles and thought they had found a cow's nest.

3 The Indefinite Article *a/an* – Der unbestimmte Artikel

3.1 Die Bildung

Der unbestimmte Artikel ***a* wird zu *an*,** wenn das darauf folgende Wort am **Beginn mit einem Vokal *(a-e-i-o-u)* gesprochen wird.**

Examples

- **an** apple
- **an** orange
- **an** answer
- **an** opera
- **an** egg
- **an** Englishman
- **an** hour
- **an** honour

ABER: a uniform ['ju:nɪfɔ:m], **a** university [ju:nɪ'vɜ:sɪtɪ], **a** union ['ju:njən] etc.

3.2 Die Verwendung

Der unbestimmte Artikel steht **nur vor zählbaren Begriffen.**

Examples

- **a** house
- **a** car
- **a** pair of jeans
- **a** piece of news

Im Unterschied zum Deutschen steht er auch

bei Angabe des Berufs, der Nationalität, Religion, Partei etc.

Examples
- I am **a taxi driver.**
- My father is **a teacher.**
- He is **an American.**
- Thomas Moore was **a Christian.**
- His wife is **a socialist.**

⚠ Er steht jedoch nicht bei Ämtern/Stellungen, die es zu einem bestimmten Zeitpunkt **nur einmal** gibt.

Examples
- DONALD TRUMP is President of the United States.
- ELIZABETH WINDSOR is Queen of England.

in bestimmten Phrasen.

Examples
- **to be in a hurry** = *in Eile sein*
- **to have a cough** = *Husten haben*
- **to have a headache** = *Kopfweh haben*
- **to have an appetite** = *Appetit haben*
- **in a loud voice** = *mit lauter Stimme*
- **it's a pity** = *es ist schade*

nach *as*.

Example
I got this **as a** present from my husband.

bei Zeit- und Maßeinheiten in der Bedeutung ‚je', ‚pro'.

Examples
- He drives at 50 miles **an** hour.
- The tomatoes are 80 p **a** pound.

Der unbestimmte Artikel steht **nach *such, half, quite*** und ***rather*** sowie nach ***so*** bzw. ***too*** **+ Eigenschaftswort.**

Examples
- **such a** silly idea
- **half an** hour
- **quite a** nice man
- **rather a** bad joke
- **so cold a** night
- **too long a** story

Your Turn: 'Indefinite Article'

Fill in ***a*** or ***an*** where necessary.

1. What ______ silly thing to do!
2. As ______ little girl, Susan wanted to become ______ vet.
3. What ______ nice furniture you have got in your new house!
4. Have you ever seen such ______ tall woman?
5. I have never heard such ______ nonsense before.
6. It is ______ great fun to play beach volleyball.
7. ______ apple ______ day keeps the doctor away.
8. That was ______ good advice.
9. "Is your friend ______ Englishman?" – "No, he isn't, he is ______ Scotsman."
10. It was such ______ bad weather that we could not go out all day.
11. "Is Mr Myers ______ plant manager?" – "No, he is ______ CEO."
12. Donald Trump became ______ president in 2017.
13. It is ______ pity that you have got ______ headache now.

14. He shouted at me in ______ loud voice.
15. Last night I had rather ______ bad nightmare.
16. Though there was ______ plenty of time and no need to be in ______ hurry, he ignored the fact that he was not allowed to drive faster than 30 miles ______ hour.
17. Are you ______ Catholic or ______ Protestant?
18. It might be quite ______ good idea to send her to university; she is such ______ bright girl.
19. He came to London as ______ boy of six. Now he is ______ true Englishman.
20. Did you get this holiday as ______ birthday present?

How can we be sure that Santa Claus is an Irishman?
Usually there are two doors in a house and about eight windows, and he goes down the chimney.

4 The Definite Article *the* – Der bestimmte Artikel

4.1 Die Bildung

Im Englischen gibt es **nur einen bestimmten Artikel *the* für alle Hauptwörter.**

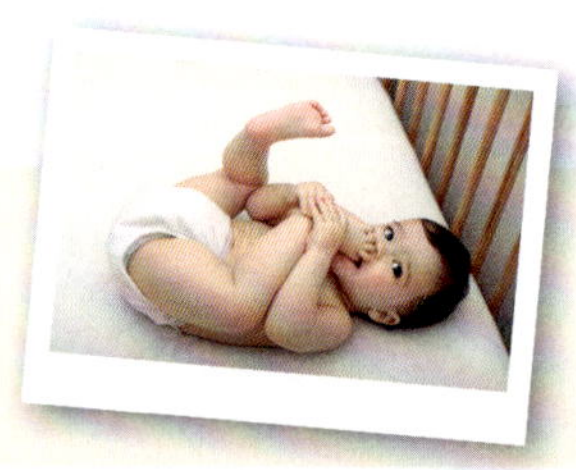

Examples
- the man
- the woman
- the child
- the dog
- the room
- the car

Wird das **darauf folgende Wort mit Vokal gesprochen *(a-e-u-o-u)*,** so **ändert sich die Aussprache des Artikels *the*** [θe] zu [θi].

Examples
- **the** answer
- **the** umbrella
- **the** island
- **the** ice cream
- **the** hour

4.2 Die Verwendung

Der **bestimmte Artikel** wird – anders als im Deutschen – **unter anderem zur Hervorhebung eines Einzelnen aus einer Menge** verwendet, oft mit **der Präposition *of*.**

Examples
- **the children** in my school
- **the people** in our street
- **the Mr Jones** in my company
- **the Queen of** England
- **the House of** Lords

Im Detail gelten die folgenden Regeln:

Ohne Artikel stehen

Eigennamen

Eigennamen, auch in Verbindung mit Titeln, Verwandtschaftsbezeichnungen oder Eigenschaftswörtern wie *good, old, young, dear, little, poor* etc.

Examples
- **Professor** Jones
- **Aunt** Mary
- **Little** John
- **Doctor** Brackets
- **Grandpa** Joe
- **Old** MacDonald

Ländernamen, auch in Verbindung mit *central, northern, modern* etc.

Examples
- Great Britain
- Italy
- Switzerland
- Iran
- **southern** France
- **modern** Greece
- **ancient** Rome

Namen von Bergen, Seen und Gewässern, außer wenn *of* folgt

Examples
- Mount McKinley
- Cape Cod
- Lake Michigan

⚠ **ABER: the** Straits **of** Gibraltar, **the** Straits **of** Dover, **the** Straits **of** Hormuz

Namen von Straßen, Brücken, Parks, Gebäuden etc.

Examples
- Oxford Street
- Fifth Avenue
- Golden Gate Bridge
- Central Park
- Tower Bridge

⚠ **ABER: the** Tower (**of** London)

Wochentage, Monatsnamen, Jahreszeiten (im Allgemeinen), **Tages- und Mahlzeiten**

Examples
- Tuesday
- March
- July
- summer
- lunch
- at night

⚠ **ABER:** in **the** morning, in **the** summer of 2010

Gattungsnamen

Gattungsnamen im Plural

Example
Horses are big animals.

Material- und Stoffbezeichnungen

Examples
- **Gold** and **silver** are metals.
- **Water, wine** and **beer** are liquids.

abstrakte Begriffe wie *time, life* etc.

Examples
- **Time** flies.
- **Life** is wonderful.

die Wörter ***school, church*** und ***hospital,*** wenn nicht das Gebäude, sondern dessen **Zweck** gemeint ist z. B. der Unterricht, der Gottesdienst

Examples
- **School** starts in September.
- Every Sunday we go to **church.**
- They had to take her to **hospital.**

⚠ **ABER:**
- **The church** is opposite **the hospital.**
- **The school** is closed in summer.

das Wort ***most*** in der Bedeutung ‚fast alle'

Examples
- **Most** people celebrate their birthday.
- **Most** children like spaghetti.

Mit Artikel stehen

Eigennamen	Gattungsnamen
Familiennamen im Plural **Examples** ■ **the** Millers ■ **the** Kennedies ■ **the** Rockefellers	**Gattungsnamen im Singular** **Example** **The** horse is a useful animal.
Ländernamen im Plural sowie **Vereinigungen und Inselgruppen** **Examples** ■ **the** Netherlands ■ **the** United Kingdom ■ **the** USA ■ **the** Soviet Union ■ **the** Orkneys ■ **the** Shetlands	**hauptwörtlich gebrauchte Eigenschaftswörter** **Examples** ■ **the** rich and **the** poor ■ **the** blind ■ **the** black ■ **the** single
Flüsse, Meere und Gebirge **Examples** ■ **the** Danube ■ **the** Thames ■ **the** North Sea ■ **the** Pacific ■ **the** Alps ■ **the** Rocky Mountains	bei **besonderer Hervorhebung von abstrakten Begriffen** wie *time, life* etc. **Examples** ■ **the** time I spent with my grandfather ■ **the** life she lived in Spain

Your Turn: 'Definite Article'

Fill in ***the*** where necessary.

1. "I'd like to see ________ Mr Summers." – "Do you mean ________ Mr Summers who works in our Human Resources department?"
2. In ________ winter of 1999 we were in ________ Switzerland; the following year we went to ________ Netherlands.
3. ________ most people think Christopher Columbus was ________ Spanish.
4. He lives in Innsbruck, but he has never been in ________ Alps.
5. ________ Mount Snowdon is in ________ Wales.
6. My grandmother is in ________ hospital until ________ Wednesday.
7. I walked along ________ Fleet Street until I reached ________ Trafalgar Square.
8. In Britain ________ tea is served with ________ milk and ________ sugar.
9. Can you remember ________ Sunday afternoon we spent together in ________ Lech on ________ Arlberg?
10. This is ________ school I went to when I was a child.
11. ________ Tower Bridge is near ________ Tower.
12. ________ elephants are ________ biggest animals I know.
13. ________ United Kingdom consists of ________ Scotland, ________ England, ________ Wales and ________ Northern Ireland.
14. ________ Danube rises in ________ Black Forest and flows into ________ Black Sea.
15. ________ most tourists want to have fun in their holidays.
16. ________ good old George died unexpectedly last night.

17. ________ Queen's residence in London is ________ Buckingham Palace.
18. ________ water boils at 100 degrees.
19. In ________ Austrian Lake District there are lots of lakes and ________ mountains. ________ highest mountain is ________ Dachstein.
20. I do not like ________ cheese we bought yesterday. I generally prefer ________ roast beef to ________ cheese.

Passenger: *"Does this bus go to Victoria?"*
Conductor: *"No."*
Passenger: *"It says so on the front."*
Conductor: *"There's an advert for baked beans on the side, but we don't sell them."*

Ziele erreicht?

Challenge 1 – Saxon Genitive

Tick the sentence if it is correct. If it is wrong, rewrite it.

	✓	×
1. Susan's and Jim's exam results were excellent.		
2. Next week's weather will be awful.		
3. Have you seen the latest film of Rosamunde Pilcher?		
4. Henry does not like his new shirt's colour.		
5. My teacher wants to see my parents at the end of the week.		
6. The dog ran along the river's bank.		
7. The police are investigating the murder of the young man.		
8. The man at the street's corner has been standing there since morning.		

Challenge 2 – Articles

Fill in the missing articles where necessary.

See 'Topics': Travelling and Tourism

________ Real Life of Maria von Trapp

Maria Augusta Kutschera was born in ________ city of Vienna, Austria, in 1905. She grew up as ________ orphan and was raised by ________ abusive relative. After finishing ________ college she entered ________ Benedictine Abbey of Nonnberg in Salzburg as ________ novice. Unfortunately, her health suffered as she did not get enough exercise and ________ fresh air. So when Georg von Trapp was seeking ________ tutor for his sick daughter, ________ Reverend Mother of ________ Abbey chose ________ Maria not only because of her training and skill as ________ teacher, but also because of ________ concern for her health.

Maria developed ________ caring and loving relationship with all ________ children. She enjoyed singing with them and getting them involved in ________ outdoor activities. When ________ Georg von Trapp asked her to stay with him and become ________ new mother to his children, she agreed. They were married in ________ church of Nonnberg Abbey in ________ year 1927. They had three children together.

During ________ worldwide depression in ________ early 1930s ________ von Trapp family lost ________ most of its wealth. It was in those days that they began considering making ________ family hobby of singing into ________ profession. ________ Georg von Trapp did not want his family to perform in ________ public, but eventually had to give in. ________ family won ________ first place in ________ Salzburg Music Festival in ________ 1936 and became quite successful all across Europe.

When ________ Nazis took over Austria and made it a part of Germany, ________ von Trapps soon became aware of ________ negative influence of ________ new political ideas and principles. ________ Georg von Trapp not only refused to fly ________ Nazi flag on their house, but he also declined ________ naval command and ________ request to sing at ________ Hitler's birthday party.

They decided to leave Austria and travelled via London to ________ USA by ship. In ________ early 1940s ________ family settled in Stowe, Vermont, where they bought ________ farm. In ________ 1950 they opened ________ Trapp Family Lodge to guests, and it is still operating today. Maria von Trapp died in 1987.

Joan Gearin – adapted

The Passive Voice – Das Passiv

Meine Ziele

Nach Bearbeitung dieses Kapitels kann ich

- das Passiv in den gebräuchlichsten Formen bilden;
- Verben aus dem Aktiv ins Passiv transferieren;
- Sätze im Passiv spontan bilden und im Kontext korrekt verwenden.

1 Die Bildung

Bei der Bildung des Passivs wird das **Objekt des aktiven Satzes zum Subjekt des Passivsatzes.** Das Verb wird hierbei ins Passiv gesetzt. Das Subjekt des aktiven Satzes kann bei Bedarf, d. h. vor allem wenn es sich um ein Hauptwort oder um einen Eigennamen handelt, mit ***by*** angefügt werden.

	Subjekt		Objekt
Active	Tom	**eats**	an apple.
Passive	An apple	**is eaten**	**by** Tom.
	Subjekt		Objekt

	Subjekt		Objekt
Active	Our children	**need**	new shoes.
Passive	New Shoes	**are needed**	**by** our children.
	Subjekt		Objekt

Das Verb wird aus der Form von ***to be* und dem Past Participle (= 3. Form)** gebildet. Falls das Verb in der Verlaufsform (= ‚*-ing*'-Form) steht, wird die Form ***being*** eingeschoben.

Hier die gebräuchlichsten Formen:

		Examples
Present Simple	*am/is/are* + Past Participle	Breakfast **is** always **made** by mum.
	can/may/must/shall + *be* + Past Participle	■ This machine **cannot be repaired.** ■ John **must be invited,** too.
Present Continuous	*am/is/are being* + Past Participle	Don't go out, the grass **is** just **being cut.**
Past Simple	*was/were* + Past Participle	His football team **was beaten** last night.
Past Continuous	*was/were being* + Past Participle	The flowers **were being watered** by the gardener when it started to rain.
Present Perfect Simple	*have/has been* + Past Participle	The job **has been finished.**
Past Perfect Simple	*had been* + Past Participle	The new front window **had been broken.**
***Will*-Future**	*will be* + Past Participle	A new restaurant **will be opened** in Sloane Street.
***Going-to*-Future**	*am/is/are going to be* + Past Participle	Your bike **is going to be repaired.**
Future Perfect	*will have been* + Past Participle	In an hour the snowboard **will have been sold** on eBay.
Conditional I	*would be* + Past Participle	Her house **would be sold** if she did not pay.
Conditional II	*would have been* + Past Participle	My garden **would have been ruined** if you had not helped me.

2 Die Verwendung

1. Das Passiv wird im Englischen häufiger verwendet als im Deutschen, vor allem dann, wenn die handelnde Person unwichtig oder gar nicht genannt ist. Es findet sich **vorrangig in der Schriftsprache,** besonders in **Berichten** und **Zeitungsartikeln.**

Examples

- Clothes are produced all over the world.
- Many people were taken to hospital after the accident.
- New houses will be built in Kingston Road.
- More and more cars would be imported from Asia.

2. Enthält ein Satz **zwei Objekte,** wird **vorzugsweise das Objekt im 3. Fall** (O_3; das ist meist eine Person) zum **Subjekt.**

	O_3 O_4
Active	My aunt **gave** me a lot of presents.
Passive	I **was given** a lot of presents.
	Subjekt O_4

Wird das Objekt im 4. Fall (= O_4) zum Subjekt, so wird das Objekt im 3. Fall mit Präposition eingefügt.

	O_3 O_4
Active	My aunt **gave** me a lot of presents.
Passive	A lot of presents **were given** to me.
	Subjekt O_3

Examples

Active	Granny **told** us a lot of stories.	Somebody **sent** him a parcel.
Passiv	■ We **were told** a lot of stories. ■ A lot of stories **were told** to us.	■ He **was sent** a parcel. ■ A parcel **was sent** to him.

Your Turn: 'Passive Voice'

Your Turn 1

Change the sentences into passive voice using the words in bold as subjects.

Model sentence
They promised **me** a new bike for Christmas. I was promised a new bike for Christmas.

1. They allowed **us** to stay. ______
2. Somebody will bring **them** flowers. ______
3. They handed **the postman** a letter. ______
4. Tom has lent **me** his book. ______
5. They had offered **her** a lot of money. ______
6. They promised **the best pupils** prizes. ______
7. Somebody sent **a friend of mine** a cake. ______
8. The teacher will show **us** a film. ______
9. Somebody has given **him** a dictionary. ______
10. We gave **them** some fish. ______
11. John has just told **me** a good story. ______
12. My father bought **me** a new bike last week. ______

3. Die **Präposition** bleibt immer **hinter dem Verb.**

Examples
- The old lady **was well looked after** in her new home.
- The dog **was not searched for** because nobody missed it.
- Talent is not enough; success **must** always **be worked for.**

Your Turn: 'Passive Voice'

Your Turn 2

Change the sentences into passive voice putting the prepositions in the correct place.

1. Everybody listened to him carefully. ______
2. The bus had run over a dog. ______
3. A good doctor will operate on him. ______
4. People were talking about the circus. ______
5. They looked for the cat everywhere. ______

6. He sent for Tom. ____________________
7. Everybody cared for the sick child. ____________________
8. Nobody has heard of him since. ____________________
9. Men must always wait for women. ____________________
10. They are just carrying out your orders. ____________________

4. Die **unpersönliche deutsche Form ‚man'** wird ebenfalls mit der Form des Passivs ausgedrückt.

Examples

- Nowadays English is spoken everywhere. – *Heutzutage spricht* ***man*** *überall Englisch.*
- Haggis is eaten in Scotland. – *In Schottland isst* ***man*** *Haggis.*
- Summer holidays are traditionally spent in Brighton. – *Den Sommerurlaub verbringt* ***man*** *traditionellerweise in Brighton.*

Your Turn: 'Passive Voice'

Your Turn 3

Translate the following 'man'-sentences.

1. Man hat mir schon mein Hotelzimmer gezeigt. ____________________
2. Man gab John gestern den ersten Preis. ____________________
3. Man schickte mir eine Menge Briefe. ____________________
4. Hat man dir das Neueste schon erzählt? ____________________
5. Man gab ihm bei der Feier ein schönes Geschenk. ____________________
6. Man gab ihnen eine neue Arbeit. ____________________
7. Hat man euch alle Zimmer gezeigt? ____________________
8. Schau, was man mir gegeben hat! ____________________
9. Wie viel Geld hat man dir geboten? ____________________
10. Man wird dir eine Menge Schwierigkeiten machen. ____________________
11. In unserer Stadt gibt man den armen Leuten gratis Essen. ____________________
12. Man hat mir den Brief nie gezeigt. ____________________

A little girl was playing in the park, when a kindly old lady started talking to her.
"And do you go to school?" she asked.
"No," was the short answer, "I am sent there!"

Ziele erreicht?

Challenge 1

Complete the following sentences using the correct passive forms of the verbs in brackets.

1. Nowadays a lot of drugs like opium and marihuana ______________________ (import) from North African countries and Afghanistan.
2. In a few decades, Denmark and The Netherlands ______________________ (flood) if the sea level rises.
3. The African Association APPBOSA ______________________ (Fairtrade certify) since the end of 2003.
4. In the former German Democratic Republic people ______________________ (watched, continuously) by the state.
5. By the end of the century, global economic barriers ______________________ (break down) completely.
6. The first primitive dishwasher ______________________ (invent) by JOSEPHINE COCHRAN in Illinois, USA in 1886.
7. Gardening ______________________ (make) popular in the USA since First Lady MICHELLE OBAMA started to grow her own vegetables in the White House gardens.
8. In the Middle Ages people ______________________ (torture) cruelly until they confessed or died.
9. With the coming of rail transit in the early 19th century, travelling ______________________ (revolutionise) as it became cheaper, easier and safer to travel.
10. In most green hotels the water ______________________ (heat) by a photovoltaic system and the food ______________________ (deliver) by local farmers.
11. International Women's Day ______________________ (celebrate) on all continents for over 100 years now.
12. In former times, children from wealthy families ______________________ (educate) by a private tutor or a governess or attended an expensive public school.

barrier = die Schranke
to torture = foltern

Challenge 2

First, read through the timeline of McDonald's. Then change it into a text using as many passive constructions as possible.

See 'Topics': Food and Trends

Start like this:

In 1955 the first McDonald's restaurant was opened in Illinois, USA. Seven years later 'The Golden Arches' …

1955 ... open the first McDonald's restaurant in Illinois, USA

1962 ... make 'The Golden Arches' their company logo

1968 ... add 'The Big Mac' to the menu

1972 ... introduce 'The Quarter Pounder'

1975 ... present the Drive-Thru concept in Oklahoma, USA

1978 ... set up the 5,000th restaurant in Japan

1984 ... establish RMCC, Ronald McDonald Children's Charities, when its founder Ray Kroc died

1986 ... open the 9,000th restaurant in Sydney, Australia

1991 ... hold McHappy Day for the first time in Australia and raise USD 375,000 for RMCC

1993 ... launch the first McCafe in Melbourne, Australia

1999 ... open the 25,000th restaurant in Chicago, USA

2006 ... introduce nutrition labelling to packaging on all products and bring attention to 'fresh foods' like fruit and salads

2009 ... start a partnership with 20th Century Fox

2012 ... open their largest restaurant in the world on the London Olympics site, where staff serve on average 100,000 portions of fries, 50,000 Big Macs and 30,000 milkshakes

nutrition labelling = die Nährwertangaben

Relative Clauses – Die Relativsätze

Meine Ziele

Nach Bearbeitung dieses Kapitels kann ich
- nicht einschränkende Relativsätze erkennen und Sprechpausen bzw. Beistriche setzen;
- die verschiedenen Relativpronomen richtig verwenden;
- erkennen, wann ich ein Relativpronomen wegfallen lassen kann.

1 Defining and Non-Defining Relative Clauses – Einschränkende und nichteinschränkende Relativsätze

Die Relativsätze dienen – wie im Deutschen – zur näheren Bestimmung eines Satzgliedes im Hauptsatz.

Das Englische unterscheidet zwei Formen:

defining/restrictive relative clauses	non-defining/non-restrictive relative clauses
Der einschränkende Relativsatz ist für das Verständnis des Hauptsatzes notwendig. Er wird immer ohne Sprechpause bzw. Komma ein- oder angefügt.	Im Gegensatz dazu enthalten ergänzende Relativsätze nur zusätzliche, erläuternde Mitteilungen. Sie werden vom Hauptsatz durch eine Sprechpause bzw. ein Komma abgegrenzt.
Examples ■ The car **that he bought** is very fast. ■ I have never met the man **who lives next door.**	**Examples** ■ My uncle Jim, **who lives in Canada,** is my mother's only brother. ■ Vienna, **which is situated on the Danube,** is the capital of Austria.

Your Turn: 'Defining and Non-Defining Relative Clauses'

Put commas where necessary. Then read out the sentences to a partner. Remember to make a pause if you have put a comma.

1. I got the tickets for the concert next Monday which will be conducted by Sir Simon Rattle.
2. The man who works in the shop around the corner is always very friendly.
3. My brother did not like the film which he watched yesterday.
4. This woman who is a ballet dancer is my colleague.
5. Schools would offer activities for pupils whose parents want them to stay in the afternoons.
6. Parents who send their children to different schools will probably welcome the new common opening hours.
7. This is the neighbour whose children give loud parties every weekend.
8. The measures that our government spoke of will be put into practice next autumn.
9. This is a serious problem and one which the government has yet to answer.
10. One thing that worries a lot of people is social networks like Facebook and Twitter.
11. This is the poor woman who we want to raise money for.
12. The last music event which was organised by famous people was a huge success.
13. This is the man whose wife has had an accident recently.
14. People listened to well-known singers who came together especially for the concert.
15. This concert which was well-attended was one of the biggest music events in our century.
16. The Prime Minister who went to the same college as my brother is facing a press conference next week.

huge = riesig
well-attended = gut besucht

2 Relative Pronouns – Die Relativpronomen

Relativsätze werden durch ein Relativpronomen eingeleitet. Man verwendet

1. ***who/whom*** für Personen und Haustiere. Der Gebrauch von *whom* beschränkt sich jedoch fast nur mehr auf Schriftstücke.

⚠ Wenn *whom* in der gesprochenen Sprache verwendet wird, klingt es sehr ‚akademisch' oder auch ‚angeberisch'. Es wird häufig verwendet, um die Bildung oder die Zugehörigkeit des Sprechers/der Sprecherin zur ‚upper class' zu demonstrieren.

Examples
- The man **who** lives next door is my sister's boy-friend.
- Simon, **who(m)** I have known for many years, works in the same company.
- My dog Lillie, **who** I got when I was ten, is my best friend.
- This is the man **who(m)** I worked for in my summer-job last year.

2. ***which*** für Dinge und Tiere (außer Haustiere) sowie für ganze Sätze.

Examples
- We reached the steps **which** led up to the second floor.
- This house, **which** is very expensive, belongs to my brother.
- The book **which** you gave me last week was a great help for the exam!
- He never wears safety goggles in the lab, **which** is rather stupid and hazardous.

3. ***whose*** für Personen und Tiere zum Ausdruck des Genitiv (deutsch: dessen/deren).

Examples
- The man **whose** name I always forget came to my office this morning.
- The dog **whose** owner is sitting on the bench is not well-trained.
- KARL MAY, **whose** thrilling books are read all over the world, was never in the Wild West.

⚠ Bei Gegenständen und Dingen wird die Konstruktion mit *with* verwendet.

Examples
- The house **with** the broken windows belongs to my grandparents.
- The car **with** the shining aluminium rims was given to me by my parents.

aluminium rim = die Alufelge

4. ***that*** für Personen, Dinge und Tiere, vor allem als Subjektform anstelle von *which;* vorzugsweise nach allen Superlativen und in der Bedeutung ähnlichen Wörtern wie *all, some(one/thing), nothing, any(one/thing), every(one/thing), first, only, much/many, little/few, none.*

⚠ Im modernen gesprochenen Englisch wird es allerdings immer weniger verwendet und meist durch ***who*** oder ***which*** ersetzt.

Examples
- The shoes **that/which** are standing in front of the door are mine.
- Where is the **nearest** shop **that** sells stamps?
- This is the **best** steak **that** I have ever eaten!
- Is there **anything** **that** needs discussing?
- He was the **only** person **that** could help us to find the way back to the hotel.

5. ***what*** leitet immer einen Subjekt-, Objekt- oder Prädikativsatz ein (deutsch: ‚... das, was ...')

Examples

- **What** she says is not important.
- **What** they want is money.
- I do not know **what** to do.
- He never listens to me – this is exactly **what** I told him yesterday.
- Tell me **what** you remember of it.

Your Turn: 'Relative Pronouns'

Fill in a suitable relative pronoun.

1. Is the book ______________ is lying on your bedside table boring or interesting?
2. Our friends, ______________ invited us over for lunch, are excellent cooks.
3. My new flatmate, ______________ comes from New Zealand, seems to be very nice.
4. I do not believe anything ______________ is written in this book.
5. We could not understand ______________ our friends had done.
6. I love and respect my father, ______________ has worked in the same company all his life.
7. Tomorrow I am seeing an old friend of mine ______________ lives in Seattle.
8. The young man is speaking a language ______________ has never been heard before.
9. She deeply regretted ______________ she had done.
10. The children, ______________ walk my dog every afternoon, are playing in the garden now.
11. The bunch of flowers ______________ is standing on the table has my favourite colours.
12. His cousin ______________ arrived last night is staying at the Ritz.

to regret = bereuen

3 Leaving out the Relative Pronoun – Der Wegfall des Relativpronomens

Wenn der Relativsatz **ein eigenes Subjekt** besitzt, kann besonders im gesprochenen Englisch das Relativpronomen weggelassen werden.

Examples

- She is the girl (who) **I** want to marry.
- Are these the oranges (that) **we** bought in the supermarket yesterday?
- That is all (that) **I** know.
- He is not the man (who) **we** used to know from school.
- This book was the only one (that) **they** had about gardening in the library.
- We will do anything (that) **you** want us to.

Your Turn: 'Leaving out the Relative Pronoun'

Fill in a suitable relative pronoun where necessary.

1. The medicine ______________ the doctor had prescribed did not help the patient.
2. The present ______________ I gave you at your birthday party was not really very expensive.
3. What was the name of your neighbour ______________ car we borrowed two weeks ago?
4. The plane ______________ had been severely damaged in the accident was soon repaired.
5. The woman ______________ bike was stolen last night is being interviewed by the police.
6. These shoes, ______________ were very expensive, are the latest fashion.
7. The neighbours ______________ invited us for dinner are very friendly.
8. The author ______________ I met at the bookshop has just published his latest novel.
9. The doctor ______________ spoke to the patient's parents is experienced.
10. The man ______________ I met downtown yesterday is a very handsome guy.
11. The police officer ______________ has arrested the criminal is a tough man.
12. The young girl ______________ lives next door loves reading SHAKESPEARE's dramas.

"I'd like some crocodile shoes, please."
"Certainly, madam, what size are your crocodiles?"

Ziele erreicht?

Challenge 1

Fill in a suitable pronoun and a comma where necessary.

1. The men ______________ were very tired stopped working.
2. The book ______________ I bought last week is really interesting.
3. Mr Smith ______________ you met yesterday evening is my new boss.
4. Mother gave the letter to Jim ______________ posted it for her.
5. Someone ______________ smokes must have been in my bedroom.
6. The Austrian ______________ name is probably best known in the United States is ARNOLD SCHWARZENEGGER.
7. Paul ______________ girlfriend is from Spain can speak Spanish quite fluently.
8. The girl ______________ mother I was talking to has just left the room.
9. The old gentleman ______________ lives across the street has got married for the third time.
10. Budapest ______________ is on the Danube is a very beautiful city.
11. The teacher reads ______________ the pupils had written on the blackboard.
12. Our new teacher ______________ name I have forgotten is from Berlin.
13. The doctor did all ______________ was necessary.
14. The River Thames ______________ flows through London is more than two hundred miles long.

15. I do not believe ______________ he has just told us.
16. In detective stories the murderer is always caught ______________ does not happen in real life.
17. The clock struck thirteen ______________ made everybody laugh.
18. Show me ______________ you have got in your hands.
19. The boy ______________ threw the stone will be punished.
20. I think this is the funniest film ______________ has ever been produced.

An old man and a young lad were sitting on opposite benches in the park. Suddenly the old man leaned across and shouted, "It's no use your talking to me from over there. I'm deaf." "I'm not talking to you," the boy shouted back. "I'm chewing bubblegum."

Challenge 2

Complete the text by filling in the missing relative pronouns.

See 'Topics': Violence in Society

More States Allowing Guns in Bars

Happy-hour beers were going for $ 5 at Past Perfect, a well-attended bar in Nashville, Tennessee, when Adam Ringenberg walked in with a loaded 9-millimeter pistol ______________ he was hiding in the front pocket of his grey trousers.

Mr Ringenberg, ______________ works as a technology consultant, is one of the state's nearly 300,000 handgun permit holders ______________ have recently seen their rights greatly expanded by a new law ______________ allows them to carry loaded firearms into bars and restaurants ______________ serve alcohol. "If someone's sticking a gun in my face, I'm not relying on their charity to keep me alive," said Mr Ringenberg, 30, ______________ said he carries the gun for personal protection when he is not at work. Gun rights advocates like Mr Ringenberg may applaud the new law, but many customers, waiters and restaurant proprietors here are shocked by the decision. "That's not okay," Art Andersen, 44, said. "It opens the door to trouble."

advocate = der/die Befürworter/in

Tennessee is one of four states, along with Arizona, Georgia and Virginia, ______________ recently enacted laws ______________ explicitly allow loaded guns in bars. Eighteen other states allow weapons in restaurants ______________ serve alcohol. The new measures in the four states come after two landmark Supreme Court rulings that citizens have an individual right to keep a loaded handgun to defend their homes. The rulings, ______________ overturned handgun bans in Washington and Chicago, have strengthened the position of the gun lobby. More than 250 legal actions now question various gun laws, and Gov. Rick Perry of Texas, ______________ argues that armed bystanders might have stopped the gunman at a shooting last week at the University of Texas in Austin, calls for guns to be made legal on campuses.

landmark ruling = eine Entscheidung, die einen Wendepunkt markiert

Malcolm Gay, The New York Times – adapted

The Reported Speech – Die indirekte Rede

Meine Ziele

Nach Bearbeitung dieses Kapitels kann ich

- Sätze von der direkten in die indirekte Rede transferieren;
- zwischen Vorzeitigkeit, Gleichzeitigkeit und Nachzeitigkeit von berichteten Situationen unterscheiden;
- die richtige Wortfolge in der indirekten Frage einhalten;
- die Infinitivkonstruktion beim indirekten Befehl korrekt bilden;
- die indirekte Rede in allen Varianten bei Berichten und eigenen Erzählungen anwenden.

1 The Reported Speech and the Reported Question – Die indirekte Rede und die indirekte Frage

1. Wenn ein Satz in der direkten Rede von einem/einer Sprecher/in wiedergegeben wird, spricht man von der ‚indirekten Rede' (= ‚reported speech'). Sie besteht aus einem **einleitenden Hauptsatz** und einem **Objektsatz.** Der Hauptsatz leitet den Objektsatz stets mit der Konjunktion ***that*** ein, vor die **kein Komma** gesetzt wird. Beim Sprechen wird sie meist weggelassen.

Hauptsatz	Objektsatz
He says **(that)** ...	he is in his office at the moment.
Konjunktion: **(that)**	

Einleitewörter (= ‚reporting verbs') sind ***say*** oder ***tell somebody*** sowie ***think, know, hope, wish, be sure, be afraid*** etc.

2. So wie im Deutschen **ändern sich die Pronomina** entsprechend der Person, die berichtet.

Examples
- Tom says, **"I** am tired." → Tom says that **he** is tired.
- Our parents say, **"We** will go out." → Our parents say that **they** will go out.
- He tells me, **"You** look great." → He tells me that **I** look great.

3. Der **indirekte Fragesatz** (= ‚reported question') kann auf unterschiedliche Art und Weise eingeleitet werden.

Einleitung wahlweise mit

ask if/ask whether	***ask*** **mit einem Fragewort, wie z. B.** ***who/what/where/when/why***	***wonder*** **(= sich fragen),** ***want to know*** **(= wissen wollen) u. ä.**
Example	**Example**	**Example**
He **asks if** we are at home.	She **asks** me **where** I have been.	I **wonder if** they will come.
Hauptsatz: He asks / Indirekter Fragesatz: if we are at home	Hauptsatz: She asks me / Indirekter Fragesatz: where I have been	Hauptsatz: I wonder / Indirekter Fragesatz: if they will come

4. Die Wortstellung im indirekten Fragesatz entspricht jener im Aussagesatz. Es gibt keine Wortumstellung (= Inversion), daher fallen die Hilfszeitwörter ***do, does*** oder ***did*** der direkten Frage weg.

Examples
- **Can you call** him? → She asks me if **I can call** him.
- **Does she like** you? → He wants to know if **she likes** me.
- **Did they buy** the house? → I ask them if **they bought** the house

5. Im Gegensatz zum Deutschen steht sowohl in der indirekten Rede als auch in der indirekten Frage das **Verb nicht im Konjunktiv** (= Möglichkeitsform), sondern **richtet sich nach der Zeitenfolge.**

Man unterscheidet folgende **zwei Varianten der Zeitenfolge:**

1. Das **‚reporting verb'** steht in der Simple- oder Continuous-Form der **Present, Present Perfect** oder **Future Tense.** In der indirekten Rede steht dann diejenige Zeitform, die auch in der direkten Rede steht. Es ändern sich nur, falls erforderlich, die Pronomina.

Examples

- Tom says, "I **want** to speak to Jim." → Tom says that he **wants** to speak to Jim.
- Sue has said, "Mum **is waiting."** → Sue has said that Mum **is waiting.**
- Frank will say, "**I've finished** my homework." → Frank will say that he **has finished** his homework.
- Bo says, "We**'ll be** in time." → Bo says that they **will be** in time.
- Joe has said, "I **went** to Fran's party last night." → Joe has said that he **went** to Fran's party last night.
- Jim will say, "I **am going to** travel to Spain soon." → Jim will say that he **is going to** travel to Spain soon.

2. Das **‚reporting verb'** steht in der Simple- oder Continuous-Form der **Past** oder **Past Perfect Tense** oder im **Conditional.** Die nachfolgenden Zeitformen werden gemäß der Zeitenfolge verändert.

Present Tense	→	**Past Tense**
Past Tense	→	**Past Perfect Tense**
Present Perfect Tense	→	**Past Perfect Tense**
Past Perfect Tense	→	**Past Perfect Tense**
Future Tense	→	**Conditional I**
Conditional I	→	**Conditional I**
Conditional II	→	**Conditional II**

a) Beim Bilden von Sätzen in der direkten Rede oder von der indirekten Frage unterscheidet man, ob die berichtete Handlung **gleichzeitig, vorzeitig oder nachzeitig** abläuft.

Gleichzeitig	‚was zum gleichen Zeitpunkt geschieht'	Past Tense
Vorzeitig	‚was vorher geschah'	Past Perfect Tense
Nachzeitig	‚was nachher geschehen wird'	Conditional I (*would* + Infinitive)
Conditional I/II	‚was geschehen könnte/hätte können'	keine Änderung

Examples

- Tom said, "I **want to speak to** Jim." → Tom said that he **wanted to speak to** Jim.
  = **gleichzeitig**
- Sue said, "Mum **is waiting."** → Sue said that Mum **was waiting.**
  = **gleichzeitig**
- Frank said, "**I've finished** my homework." → Frank said that he **had finished** his homework.
  = **vorzeitig**
- Bo said, "We**'ll be** in time." → Bo said that they **would be** in time.
  = **nachzeitig**
- Joe said, "I **went** to Fran's party on Monday." → Joe said that he **had gone** to Fran's party on Monday.
  = **vorzeitig**

⚠ Jim said, "I **am going to** buy a new bike soon." → Jim said that he **was going to** buy a new bike soon.

„ich beabsichtige" = **gleichzeitig**

b) Wenn das **‚reporting verb'** in einer **vergangenen Zeit** oder dem **Conditional** steht, kann vor allem in der gesprochenen Sprache auch die **Present Tense** verwendet werden, wenn
- es sich um eine **Aussage** handelt, die **allgemein gültig** ist
- es sich um eine **Gewohnheit** handelt oder
- die Handlung auch **in der Gegenwart wahr** ist.

Examples
- Our teacher **said** that the earth **moves** around the sun.
- She **told** me that she **goes swimming** regularly.
- My aunt **told** us that London is a cosmopolitan and lively city.
- Tom **said** that his wife **is** in hospital. *(She is still in hospital.)*

c) Wenn die Handlung nicht am selben Tag berichtet wird, also der Zeitraum des Berichtens nicht ident ist mit jenem in der direkten Rede, so ändern sich sinngemäß auch die verwendeten **Zeitangaben** („Heute ist morgen schon gestern."). Dasselbe gilt für **Ortsangaben.**

now	→	then
today	→	that day
here	→	there
this	→	that
these	→	those
ago	→	before
last week/month/year	→	the week/month/year before
yesterday	→	the day before
the day before yesterday	→	two days before
tomorrow	→	the next day/the following day
the day after tomorrow	→	in two days' time
next week/month/year	→	the following week/month/year

Your Turn: 'Reported Speech/Reported Question'

Your Turn 1

Change the following sentences into reported speech.

1. Tom said to me, "I will wait for you at the train station."
2. Pat asked me, "What are you going to do tomorrow?"
3. Jason says, "I want to be a famous actor when I have grown up."
4. Mr Smith told his secretary, "You can phone from this office."
5. Pat said, "I am living with my parents at present, but I hope that I will have my own flat soon."
6. Jill said, "I usually take my dog for a walk after work."
7. He asked me, "Have you ever met her before?"
8. Mary said, "The party last Saturday was great. We were dancing all night long."
9. Lucy said, "In this village nothing ever happens."
10. Tim said, "I have missed my train. So I will be late for work today."
11. The shop assistant said, "The sales already started last weekend."
12. Father says to John, "Tomorrow we are going to meet Granny."
13. Sue asked Ann, "Did you like your last holiday?"
14. Mr Johnson asked, "May I use your phone, sir?"
15. Father told mum, "You do not have to water the flowers. I have already done it for you."
16. Paul said, "I have just bought a new car."

Your Turn 2

You are meeting Susan, a friend from the United States. Here is the news she tells you.

1. I am living in Chicago now, and I have a partner called Bill.
2. My mother has been seriously ill for some time.
3. Sharon and Tim are getting married next July.
4. Sharon has just had a baby.
5. I do not know what Sharon's sister does.
6. I saw her with a guy I do not know at a party last week.
7. You can come and see me whenever you want to.
8. I have not seen Philip for a long time.
9. I am really enjoying my job.
10. Someone broke into my car a few weeks ago.
11. I will tell Bill that we met and give him your regards.
12. I wonder when you are going to visit me in Chicago.

On the next day you write an email to your mutual friend Fiona to inform her about the news Susan told you the day before.

mutual = gemeinsam

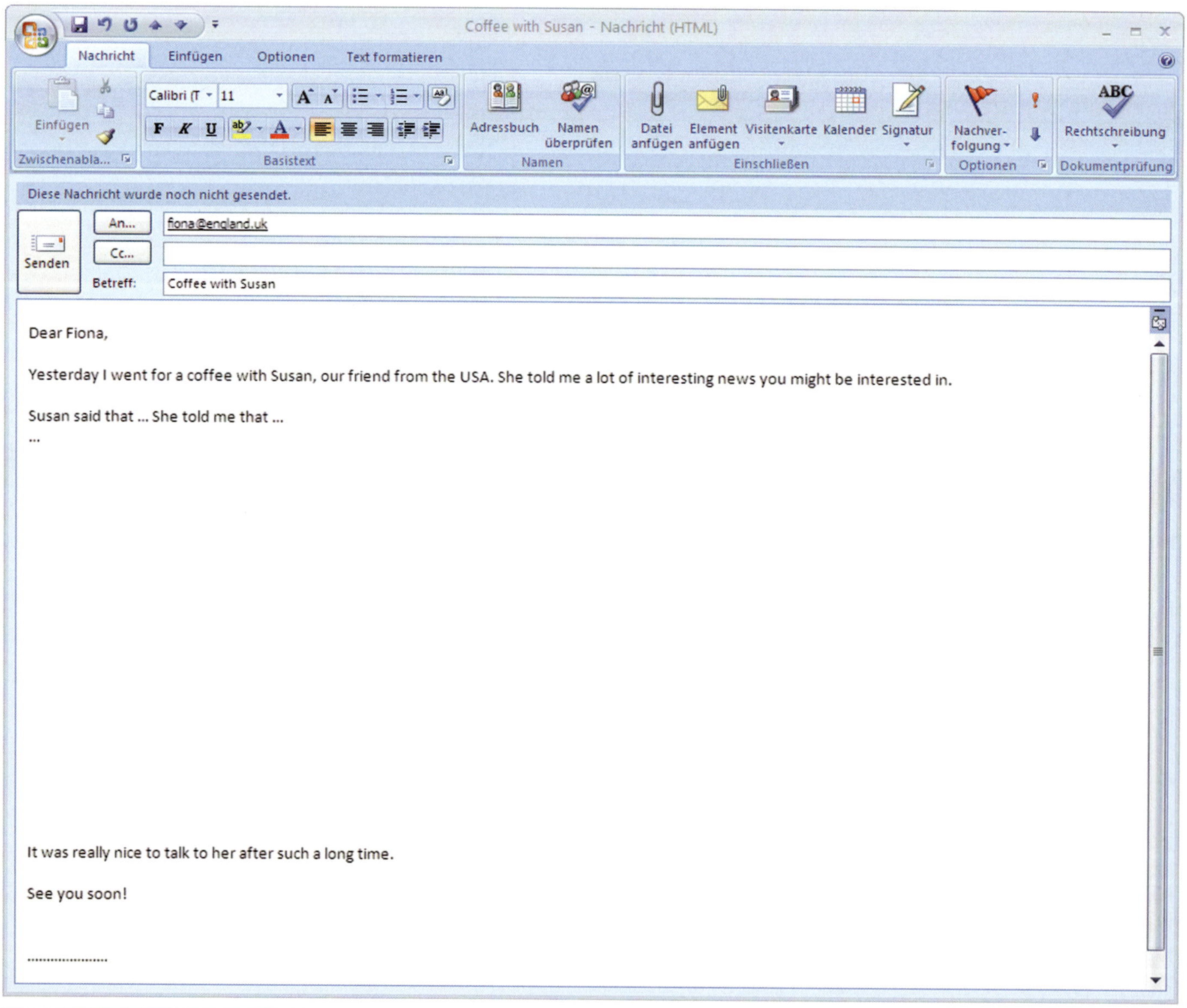

2 The Reported Command – Der indirekte Befehl

Mit Einleitewörtern wie ***tell, ask*** oder ***beg*** kann ein **indirekter Befehl** oder eine **Bitte** ausgedrückt werden. Im Gegensatz zur indirekten Rede oder Frage folgt danach – wie im Deutschen – **der Infinitiv.**

Examples

- The doctor **said to me, "Stay** in bed for a few days." → The doctor **told me to stay** in bed for a few days.
- Mum **said, "Do not go** to work." → Mum **told me not to go** to work.
- Alice **said to her husband, "Come** home quickly!" → Alice **asked her husband to come** home quickly.
- Ann **begged, "Auntie, please, don't tell** Mum!" → Ann **begged her aunt not to tell** her mother.

Your Turn: 'Reported Command'

Complete the sentences with expressions from the box.

to be careful ▪ to marry him ▪ to come to our party ▪ to worry so much ▪ to help me with the packing ▪ to open the door for me ▪ to slow down a bit ▪ to speak up

1. I was carrying two heavy bags. So I asked my neighbour ______.
2. Lydia was driving too fast. So I begged her ______.
3. Tim was very much in love with Janis. So he asked her ______.
4. Molly had difficulty understanding Jane. So she ordered her ______.
5. Dora was very pessimistic about her situation. So I told her not ______.
6. I was moving house, and here was still a lot of work left. So I asked some friends ______ ______.
7. He wanted to go climbing in the mountains. So we warned him ______.
8. They did not know anybody. So we asked them ______.

The boss of the company told the new trainee that if he was going to work in this firm, one thing he would have to learn is that they were keen on cleanliness there.
He asked him if he had wiped his feet on the mat as he came in.
"Oh yes, sir." the young man answered.
"And another thing we are keen on is truthfulness: there is no mat." the boss answered.

Ziele erreicht?

Challenge 1

Change the following sentences into reported speech.

1. "I want to go to town with my sister."

   Susan said ______.

2. "Did you recognise him by his voice?"

   They asked me ______.

3. "Mother bought herself a new evening dress the day before yesterday."
   I already knew ______________________________.
4. "Could you buy me a new TV tomorrow?"
   Granny asked me ______________________________.
5. "We are going to have a big party at the weekend."
   My friends said ______________________________.
6. "You should eat less meat and drink more water."
   The doctor told her ______________________________.
7. "I sent you an email late at night yesterday."
   Oliver's assistant informed him ______________________________.
8. "Why did you not tell the stranger the way?"
   The girl asked her boyfriend ______________________________.
9. "At the moment I am not working hard enough."
   Christy knew ______________________________.
10. "She prefers oranges to bananas."
   Her mother thought ______________________________.
11. "Has he added a message for me?"
   She hoped ______________________________.
12. "Hurry up, please, if you want to go to the theatre with me."
   Ginger asked her husband ______________________________.

Challenge 2

You work in a well-known Austrian food processing company. Your boss, who is British, sent you to a meeting with a customer in Italy. Back at the company you have to report to your boss, who only speaks English. Use the notes you have taken and tell him what you were talking about.

See 'Topics': Communication and the Media

food processing = die Lebensmittelverarbeitung

Start your sentences like this:

Our customer said that ... They told me that ... They asked if ... etc.

They want to return 3 pallets of vinegar because the shelf life is too short. They were very satisfied with the excellent quality of our wafers and baked goods. They need 20 pallets of cloudy apple juice by the end of week 36. In addition, they are thinking about ordering more cakes and biscuits if we give them a discount. They will order the same amount of cranberry juice at Christmas as last year.
This summer they sold less sparkling water, as it was extremely hot and people preferred to drink tap water. They asked about any new products in the energy drinks sector. Their boss is going to contact you next week.

vinegar = der Essig
shelf-life = die Lagerfähigkeit
wafer = das Wafferl
cloudy = naturtrüb

tap water = das Leitungswasser

Challenge 3 – 'Water Security'

See 'Topics': Ruining Our Planet

You work as an assistant for PROFESSOR GUPPINGER, a well-known scientist at Vienna University of Natural Resources and Life Sciences. Together with two other experts from the USA he has done intensive research on global water security.

University of Natural Resources and Life Sciences = die Universität für Bodenkultur (BOKU)

In an article for the English supplement of 'Der Standard' you present what PROFESSOR GUPPINGER and his colleagues have found out. **Use the following statements to write the report.**

'Human Impact on World's Rivers Threatens Water Security of 5 Billion'

Professor Alois Guppinger, University of Natural Resources and Life Sciences, Austria:
"We have found water security and biodiversity severely damaged. The world's rivers are so badly affected by human intervention that the water security of almost 5 billion people and the survival of thousands of aquatic species are in danger. Globally between 10,000 and 20,000 aquatic wildlife species are at risk or face extinction because of the human degradation of global rivers"

Professor Peter McIntyre, University of Michigan, USA:
"We were all surprised by the level of threat posed to wildlife in rich countries. What made our jaws drop is that some of the highest threat levels in the world are in the United States and Europe. Americans tend to think water pollution problems are pretty well under control, but we still face enormous challenges. The world's least affected rivers are those furthest from populated areas, such as isolated parts of the tropics, Siberia and elsewhere in the polar regions."

Professor Charles Vörösmarty, City University of New York, USA:
"The impact on wildlife in developed countries is the result of river systems that had been heavily engineered and changed by man. With all the protection the EU has in place, it was surprising to see that it was a hotspot for biodiversity loss. But for a long time Europeans have altered their landscapes, including the removal of 90 % of wetlands and floodplains, which are crucial parts of river ecosystems. Even the Amazon, which has been considered to be relatively pristine, has human fingerprints on it. While it is in generally good shape, in the upstream regions, such as Peru, there are many high density areas of people that injected threat into the system. The consequences of that human threat pass downstream into the remote forested areas of the river. My colleagues and I, we really hope the global report will highlight the need to address the actual reasons for the degradation of rivers. We are spending trillions of US dollars to fix a problem we have created in the first place. It would be much cheaper to treat the causes rather than the symptoms, which is what we do in the developed world today."

ADAM VAUGHAN, THE GUARDIAN – ADAPTED

A man was walking down the street when he saw a little boy with a dog.
He asked him if his dog bit. The boy shook his head.
The man bent down to pat the dog and was immediately bitten.
"I thought you said your dog didn't bite," he complained.
"Sure," said the boy, "but this isn't my dog."

pat = tätscheln

The Tenses – Die Zeitformen

Meine Ziele

Nach Bearbeitung dieses Kapitels kann ich

- die Simple- und Continuous-Formen in Bildung und Verwendung voneinander unterscheiden;
- die verschieden Zeiten und Zeitformen richtig bilden und in Gesprächssituationen anwenden;
- alle Zeiten im Kontext entsprechend anwenden.

1 Simple and Continuous (= Progressive) Forms – Die einfache Form und die Dauerform

1.1 Allgemeines

Die Zeiten im Englischen stimmen **nicht** mit den Formen in der österreichischen Umgangssprache überein. Daher ist es notwendig, die **Regeln** genau zu kennen, um sie richtig anwenden zu können.

Der deutlichste Unterschied zum Deutschen besteht in der Verwendung der **Verlaufsform** in den verschiedenen Zeiten.

Man verwendet

die einfache Form (= ‚Simple-Form')	die Verlaufsform (‚Continuous- bzw. Progressive-Form')
für Tatsachen, Gewohnheiten und wiederholte Handlungen.	für eine zeitlich begrenzte Handlung, die gerade stattfindet oder zu einem bestimmten Zeitpunkt in der Vergangenheit abgelaufen ist.

1.2 Die Besonderheiten

Statische Verben, die keinen Verlauf ausdrücken können, und Verben, die an sich einen **dauerhaften Zustand** anzeigen, stehen normalerweise in der ‚Simple-Form'. Dazu gehören:

1. Verben der Sinneswahrnehmung.

- see
- hear
- smell
- taste
- feel
- notice
- realise

2. Verben, die einen Zustand oder ein Besitzverhältnis ausdrücken.

- seem
- consist of *(= bestehen aus)*
- contain *(= enthalten)*
- belong to *(= gehören)*
- own
- possess
- believe
- know
- remember
- think *(= meinen, glauben)*
- understand

3. Verben, die keine Dauer ausdrücken können, weil sich die Handlung auf einen Augenblick beschränkt.

- break
- burst
- drop *(= fallen lassen)*
- smash
- crash
- hit
- enter

Manche dieser Verben können allerdings in einer anderen Bedeutung auch in der Verlaufsform stehen.

Examples
- I am having lunch right now. – *zu Mittag essen*
- We are having a party at the weekend. – *eine Party machen*
- He is thinking about buying a new car. – *überlegen*
- She is tasting the soup. – *kosten*

4. Verben, die einen Wunsch oder eine Vorliebe ausdrücken.

- like
- dislike
- love
- hate
- want
- wish

5. Verben in Handlungsfolgen, d. h. verschiedene Handlungen laufen hintereinander ab.

Example
In the morning I get up at 6 o'clock. First I go to the bathroom and have a quick shower. Then I dress and prepare breakfast for myself and my partner. After that, I brush my teeth and comb my hair.

2 Present Forms

2.1 Present Tense Simple

Die Bildung

1. Die Present Tense Simple entspricht dem **Infinitiv ohne *to*.**

Examples
- to sing – I sing
- to run – you run
- to play – we play
- to dance – they dance

2. Bei ***he/she/it*** ein **‚-*s*'** muss mit!

Examples
- he talk**s**
- she smile**s**
- it rain**s**

3. Nach Zischlauten wie [s], [z], [ʃ] und [ʒ] wird die Endung **‚-*es*'** an den Infinitiv angehängt, ebenso bei den Verben ***go*** and ***do.***

Examples
- to kiss – he kiss**es**
- to wash – she wash**es**
- to buzz – it buzz**es**
- to go – he go**es**
- to do – she do**es** [dʌz]

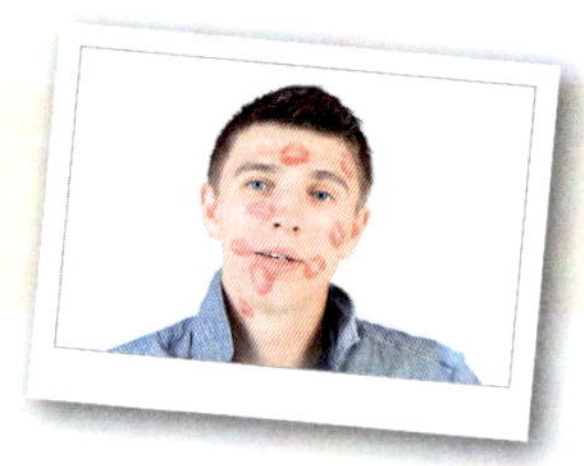

4. In der Schreibung wird **‚-*y*'** + **‚*s*'** zu **‚-*ies*',** wenn ein Konsonant davor steht.

Examples
- to fly – fl**ies**
- to cry – cr**ies**

⚠ **ABER:**
- to pla**y** – pla**ys**
- to sa**y** – sa**ys**

5. Das Verb ***to be*** hat in der 3. Person die Form ***is*** und zusätzlich für die 1. Person die Form ***am.***

Examples
- He **is** a clown.
- She **is** a pop-star.
- It **is** a boy.
- I **am** a doctor.

6. Die Hilfszeitwörter ***can, may, must, shall*** und ***will*** stehen **ohne ‚-*s*'.**

Examples
- he **can** sing
- he **may** come in
- she **must** learn
- she **shall** go
- he **will** leave

Die Verneinung (= Negation)

Sie wird mit dem Hilfszeitwort ***do*** + ***not*** bzw. bei ***he/she/it*** mit ***does*** + ***not*** gebildet, wobei beim Verb das **‚-*s*'** wegfällt.

Examples
- I play football. → I **do not play** football.
- She speaks English. → She **does not speak** English.

Kommt im Satz bereits ein **Hilfszeitwort *(be, can, may, must, shall, will, need)*** vor, so wird an dieses bei der Verneinung ***not*** angehängt.

⚠ Die Verneinung von ***must*** ist ***need not. Must not*** bedeutet *„du darfst nicht"* und drückt ein strenges Verbot aus.

Examples

- He can travel to London. → He **cannot** travel to London.
- You may enter this room. → You **may not** enter this room.
- We must be on time today. → We **need not** be on time today.

Your Turn: 'Present Forms'

Your Turn 1

Negate the following sentences.

1. They spend a lot of money. ______
2. He lives in this house. ______
3. You read well. ______
4. She feels so bad. ______
5. He sells good cakes. ______
6. We are very late. ______
7. It tastes good. ______
8. He takes English lessons. ______
9. You can wait here. ______
10. They go to the theatre. ______
11. She is French. ______
12. It costs a pound. ______

Die Frage (= Question)

Sie wird wie die Verneinung mit einem Hilfszeitwort gebildet:

mit *do* bzw. bei *he/she/it* mit *does*

Das ‚-*s*' beim Verb fällt in diesem Fall weg.

Examples

- They play football. → **Do** they **play** football?
- She speaks English. → **Does** she **speak** English?
- We love gardening. → **Do** you **love** gardening?

mit *am/is/are, can, may, must, shall, will*

Das jeweilige Hilfszeitwort wird an den Satzanfang gestellt.

Examples

- **Am** I right?
- **Is** Tom at home tonight?
- **Are** you crazy?
- **Can** he travel to London?
- **May** we enter the lawn?
- **Shall** I help you?
- **Must** we spend so much money?
- **Will** you come to my party?

Die **Fragewörter *who, what, where, when, how*** etc. stehen an erster Stelle.

Examples
- **Who** do you go to the party with?
- **What** is the time?
- **Where** are we?
- **When** do you get up?
- **How** old is she?

⚠ **Fragen nach dem Subjekt** mit ***what*** oder ***who*** stehen immer **ohne *do*.** Beide Formen verlangen hier immer ein Verb in der 3. Person Singular mit **‚-*s*'.**

Examples
- **Who goes** to school by bus?
- **What flies** south in winter?

Your Turn: 'Present Forms'

Your Turn 2

Change the following sentences into yes-/no-questions.

Model sentence
They visit their grandparents every week. *Do they visit their grandparents every week?*

1. They spend a lot of money. ______
2. He lives in this house. ______
3. You read well. ______
4. She feels well. ______
5. He sells good cakes. ______
6. They are very late. ______
7. It tastes good. ______
8. He takes English lessons. ______
9. You can wait here. ______
10. They go to the theatre. ______
11. She is French. ______
12. It costs a pound. ______

Why do cows wear bells? – Because their horns don't work.

horn = auch: die Hupe

Die Verwendung

Die Present Tense Simple wird verwendet

für Gewohnheiten und Handlungen, die sich wiederholen oder nie eintreten.	für Tatsachen und Naturgesetze.
Examples ■ The bus leaves at 6:30. ■ PRINCE CHARLES **always** has his morning tea in bed. ■ I **always** clean my house before Christmas. ■ The QUEEN **never** goes shopping alone.	**Examples** ■ The USA fights for democracy all over the world. ■ The sun rises in the east and sets in the west.

Signalwörter: *sometimes, always, ever, never, generally, usually, often, rarely, seldom* etc.

⚠ Manche Signalwörter können auch eine andere Zeit angeben (z. B. *ever, never*). Man sollte sich daher nie völlig darauf verlassen. In vielen Sätzen kommt überhaupt kein Signalwort vor.

Your Turn: 'Present Forms'

Your Turn 3

Fill in the correct forms of the verbs in brackets.

1. My brother William ______________ (not speak) German well.
2. The sun ______________ (rise) early in summer.
3. Careless driving ______________ (cause) a lot of accidents.
4. I ______________ (not like) tea with milk and sugar.
5. We rarely ______________ (spend) our weekends at home.
6. The museum ______________ (open) at 9 am and ______________ (close) at 4.30 pm.
7. My friends ______________ (have) a big cottage in Yorkshire.
8. At the weekend she ______________ (not get up) before 10 am.
9. My sister always ______________ (make) a mess in my room.
10. My boyfriend's mother often ______________ (bake) a cake on Sundays.
11. During the week I ______________ (get up) at six in the morning, but at weekends I ______________ (not get up) before 8 am.
12. At weekends, my father sometimes ______________ (go) to a football match.
13. Mother ______________ (not mow) the lawn. Father did it yesterday.
14. In order to keep fit Paula ______________ (go) jogging twice a week. Sue never ______________ (do) any sport, and she ______________ (not go) to the gym, either.

Why do doctors and nurses wear masks?
So that if somebody makes a mistake, no one will know who did it!

Your Turn 4

This is a description of Joan's daily office routine. She works as a secretary in the HR (= Human Resources) department of a multinational company.

See 'Topics': Worlds of Work

Complete the text with the correct simple forms of the matching verbs from the box.

answer ■ arrive ■ assist ■ be ■ check ■ clock in ■ clock out ■ deal with ■ discuss ■ does (2x) ■ drive ■ enter ■ finish ■ get back ■ get into ■ go (2x) ■ have (2x) ■ leave ■ organise ■ park ■ respond ■ start up ■ store ■ switch off ■ take (2x) ■ walk

In the morning she ______________ (ankommen) at the company at 7.50 and ______________ (parken) her car. She ______________ (hineingehen) the main building, ______________ (die Zeit abstempeln) and ______________ (nehmen) the lift to the third floor.

In her office she ______________ (gehen) to her desk and ______________ (hochfahren) the computer. Then she ______________ (kontrollieren) her emails and ______________ (eine Antwort schicken) if necessary.

At about 9 am she ______________ (besprechen) the daily schedule with her boss. At 10 am she ______________ (machen) a break. She usually ______________ (trinken/essen) coffee and a light snack. Then she ______________ (machen) the paperwork, ______________ (entgegennehmen) phone calls, ______________ (entgegennehmen) messages and ______________ (bearbeiten) complaints.

At 11.30 she ______________ (gehen) to the canteen to have lunch with Jenny, her colleague from the purchasing department. They ______________ (sein) good friends.

At 12.15 she ______________ (zurückkommen) from lunch. She ______________ (machen) more paperwork, ______________ (einteilen) meetings for her boss and ______________ (unterstützen) him with any tasks he needs help with.

At 16.50 she ______________ (beenden) work. She ______________ (speichern) the data and ______________ (ausschalten) her computer. Then she ______________ (zu Fuß gehen) downstairs, ______________ (die Zeit abstempeln) and ______________ (verlassen) the company. She ______________ (einsteigen) her car and ______________ (mit dem Auto fahren) home.

HR department = die Personalabteilung
to clock in/out = die Zeit abstempeln
schedule = der Terminplan
complaint = die Beschwerde
purchasing department = die Einkaufsabteilung

2.2 Present Tense Continuous

Die Bildung

Die Present Continuous wird gebildet mit ***am, is*** oder ***are*** und dem Present Participle (= **Infinitive** + **,*-ing*'**).

Examples
- I **am singing.**
- You **are flying.**
- He **is climbing.**
- We **are looking.**
- They **are protesting.**

Besonderheiten:

Das ,*-e*' am Wortende entfällt.

Examples
- to dance → dancing
- to come → coming

Konsonanten nach kurzem Vokal werden verdoppelt.

Examples
- to run → running
- to hop → hopping

Verben auf ,*-ie*' nach einem Konsonant enden auf ,*-ying*'.

Examples
- to lie → lying
- to die → dying

Die Frage und die Verneinung

Die Frage wird einfach durch Wortumstellung (= Inversion) gebildet.

Examples
- **Is he coming** home late today?
- **Are you taking** a bath?

Für die Verneinung wird *not* zwischen *am/is/are* und das Present Participle gestellt.

Examples
- **We are not going** for a holiday this year.
- **He is not cleaning** his car today.

Die Verwendung

Die Present Continuous wird verwendet

1. für Handlungen, die zum Zeitpunkt des Sprechens gerade ablaufen.

Signalwörter: *now, at this moment, still, just, look, listen, watch out, be careful* etc.

Examples
- **At the moment** Mary is preparing lunch for her family.
- **Look,** Tom is sitting in the car next to us!

2. für Handlungen, die zwar nicht gerade im Moment des Sprechens im Gange sind, aber in der Gegenwart geschehen.

Examples
- I am learning Latin at school this year.
- She is reading 'Matilda' by ROALD DAHL, and if it is good, I will read it, too.

3. für Ausnahmen von einer Gewohnheit.

Examples
- We usually get up at 7 am, but as it is Sunday, we are not getting up before 9 o'clock.
- I am actually a teacher, but as I cannot find a job, I am working as a taxi-driver.

4. mit *always, all the time* etc. als Ausdruck der Verärgerung.

Examples
- Oh dear, he is **always** buying too much beer!
- This terrible dog is running after me **all the time.**

5. für Termine und mit jemandem fest vereinbarte Handlungen in der Zukunft.

Examples
- I am seeing my boss tomorrow.
- They are having a birthday party on Saturday.

Your Turn: 'Present Tense Continuous'

Your Turn 1

Fill in the correct forms of the verbs in brackets.

1. Please, do not make such noise. I ____________ (work).
2. "Where is Tom?" – "He ____________ (wash) father's car."
3. ____________ (your Spanish, get) better?
4. John is never satisfied. He ____________ (always, complain).
5. I am tired. I ____________ (go) to bed right now.
6. Don't knock at her door. She ____________ (study) for the exam.
7. We ____________ (build) a house. We hope we will be able to finish it before November.
8. "____________ (he, work) this week?" – "No, he is on holiday."
9. ____________ (you, enjoy) the party?
10. She ____________ (have) dinner at the moment. Can you call her later?
11. Watch out! Two children ____________ (cross) the street.
12. We can go out now. It ____________ (not snow) anymore.
13. Maria is in Britain at the moment. She ____________ (learn) English there.
14. You ____________ (always, watch) TV. You should be much more active.

Your Turn 2

Look carefully at PIETER BRUEGEL's painting of a banquet at a 'Country Wedding'. What are the people in the picture doing?

PIETER BRUEGEL THE ELDER, Dutch painter (1525–1569)

Now complete the text with the correct continuous forms of the appropriate verbs in the box.

See 'Topics': Social Ties

begin ■ carry ■ celebrate ■ drink ■ eat ■ hold ■ lick ■ lie ■ look ■ pass ■ play ■ pour ■ sit (2x) ■ stand ■ stick ■ take ■ try ■ wear (2x)

to pour = schütten

The party __________ (1) place in a big barn. A lot of guests __________ (2) on simple benches around a long table. They are dressed in their festive clothes, and all of them __________ (3) hats or caps. The bride __________ (4) in the centre with her hands folded. Everybody __________ (5), __________ (6) and __________ (7).

barn = die Scheune

On a wooden door two men with white aprons __________ (8) in some plates filled with food, while another __________ (9) beer into a smaller jug. One of the guests __________ (10) the plates to the table. A dog __________ (11) his head out from under the table. Two musicians __________ (12) opposite the bride. One of them __________ (13) the bagpipes, while the other __________ (14) at the filled plates hungrily.

apron = die Schürze

jug = der Krug

bagpipes = der Dudelsack

In the foreground there is a child who __________ (15) an almost empty plate and __________ (16) its fingers. It __________ (17) a cap much too large for its head. A piece of bread __________ (18) on its lap.

lap = der Schoß

In the background a lot more people __________ (19) to get in. The party __________ (20) just __________ (21).

A motorist is driving down a one-way street the wrong way.
He is stopped by a police officer on a motorbike.
Police officer: *"Do you know where you are going?"*
Driver: *"Yes, but I must be very late. Everyone else is coming back."*

Ziele erreicht?: ‚Present Simple or Continuous?'

Fill in the correct forms of the verbs in brackets.

1. The Millers ________________ (leave) for New Zealand next Friday. Every year they ________________ (stay) there in an eco-friendly hotel for three weeks.
2. Richard says he ________________ (read) a fantastic book at the moment. I ________________ (want) to read it too when he has finished.
3. The sun ________________ (rise) in the east and ________________ (set) in the west. That is the law of nature.
4. Nowadays more and more women ________________ (bring) up their children without a father. The number of single mothers ________________ (rise) steadily.
5. Tom ________________ (take) driving lessons this week. He ________________ (have, already) a car of his own.
6. "Hi, Jack! What ________________ (you, do) here?" – "I ________________ (buy) some fish and vegetables for dinner. I ________________ (do, always) the shopping on Saturdays."
7. John ________________ (speaks) Spanish, French and English. He is really interested in foreign languages; he ________________ (learn) German this year.
8. "What ________________ (you, do)?" – "I ________________ (be) a mechanic. I ________________ (work) at a big garage in the centre of Salisbury."
9. "Listen! Someone ________________ (try) to get into our house." – "Oh no, it is only Fido, our hamster. He ________________ (make, always) a lot of noise when he ________________ (be) awake during the night."
10. This robot ________________ (drive) faster than anybody else. Unfortunately he ________________ (not work) at the moment.
11. "You ________________ (look) happy. What is going on?" – "I ________________ (think) about Peter. He is so nice. He ________________ (take) me out on Saturday. We ________________ (go) to the hottest club in town."
12. A lot of teenagers ________________ (have) problems with their parents. They ________________ (want) to be independent and to go out at weekends.
13. My brother ________________ (teach) maths and physics at grammar school. After nine years he ________________ (think) about taking a sabbatical.
14. "Why ________________ (Brian, run) so fast?" – "He ________________ (try) to catch the bus. He ________________ (take, always) the 7 o'clock bus to work."

sabbatical ≈ die Bildungskarenz

3 Future Tenses

Es gibt im Englischen verschiedene Möglichkeiten, die Zukunft auszudrücken. Die Unterschiede sind allerdings nicht immer klar und einfach zu beschreiben. Oft, aber nicht immer, haben zwei verschieden Formen eine sehr ähnliche Bedeutung.

3.1 Die *Going-to*-Future

Die Bildung

Sie wird gebildet mit ***am/is/are*** und ***going to*** und dem **Infinitiv des Verbs (ohne *to*).**

Examples
- **I am going to sing.**
- He **is going to walk.**
- They **are going to come.**

Die **Frage** wird durch **Wortumstellung (= Inversion)** gebildet. Für die Verneinung wird ***not*** zwischen ***am/is/are*** und ***going*** gestellt.

Examples
- **"Are they going to come?"** – "No, **they are** not **going to come** tonight."

Besonderheiten siehe Present Continuous, Seite 101

Die Verwendung

Die *Going-to*-Future wird verwendet

für Absichten, persönliche Entscheidungen und Pläne über Handlungen und Ereignisse in der Zukunft.

Examples
- This year I am going to eat fewer sweets.
- My sister is going to be an architect.
- From now on, we are going to study for the exam every day.

für Ereignisse, die in der Zukunft mit ziemlicher Sicherheit eintreten werden, weil ihre Anzeichen bereits in der Gegenwart erkennbar sind.

Examples
- Look at those clouds! It is going to rain soon.
- With this score of 27:9, the Dodgers are going to win anyway.
- She is going to faint; her face is as white as a sheet.

⚠ Für Termine und mit jemandem fest vereinbarte Handlungen in der Zukunft verwendet man die Present Continuous (siehe Seite 101).

Examples
- I **am seeing** Jim on Friday.
- We **are having** pasta for dinner.
- What **are** you **doing** this evening?

3.2 Die *Will*-Future

Die Bildung

Sie wird gebildet mit dem Hilfszeitwort ***will*** und dem **Infinitiv des Verbs ohne *to*.**

Examples
- **I will sing.**
- He **will walk.**
- They **will dance.**

Die **Frage** wird durch **Wortumstellung (= Inversion)** gebildet. Für die **Verneinung** wird ***not*** zwischen ***will*** und den **Infinitiv** gestellt.

Examples
"Will you marry her?" – "No, I **will not marry** this girl."

Die Verwendung

Das Englische ist in der Verwendung des Futurs konsequenter als das Deutsche, das oft das **Präsens** für eine zukünftige Handlung verwendet, z. B. Ich glaube nicht, dass ich zur Party **komme.**

Die *will*-Future wird verwendet

für ein zukünftiges Geschehen, das der/die Sprecher/in nicht beeinflussen kann.

Examples
- Easter holidays will start next Monday.
- Susan will be in Paris next week.

für eine nicht geplante Handlung und eine aus der Situation heraus spontane Entscheidung.

Examples
- We will have white wine with the fish.
- That suitcase looks heavy; I will help you with it.

in Beziehung auf etwas Künftiges bei Signalwörtern wie *think, hope, be afraid, expect, suppose* etc. und *probably, maybe* etc.

Examples
- He **thinks** his team will win the match.
- We **are sure** you will like the film.
- I **expect** he will be back soon.
- He will **probably** be late again.

Your Turn: '*Will, Going-to* or Present Continuous?'

Fill in the correct forms of the words in brackets.

1. A: "Why are you turning on the radio?" – B: "I ______________________ (listen) to the news."
2. The dancing club ______________________ (have) its summer party in July.
3. The weather is wonderful today. Before going outside, you tell your friend: "The weather is too nice to stay indoors. I ______________________ (have) a picnic in the park." – She answers: "You're right. I think I ______________________ (join) you."
4. A: "Oh, my bike has a flat tyre." – B: "Oh, really? Wait a minute. I ______________________ (help) you to push the bike home."
5. A: "I suddenly feel so dizzy." – B: "Sit down, I ______________________ (get) you a glass of water."
6. A: "The railings of the bridge do not look very safe, do they?" – B: "No, that part over there looks as if it ______________________ (fall) down soon."
7. A: "Have you sent me the email we talked about yesterday?" – B: "Oh, I'm sorry. I completely forgot. I ______________________ (send) it to you now."
8. A: "Has Sylvia decided what to do after her A-levels?" – B: "Oh, yes. She ______________________ (travel) around Australia for five weeks, and then she ______________________ (go) to university."

9. A: "What would you like to drink, sir?" – B: "I ______________ (have) a pint of cider, please."
10. The Prime Minister ______________ (arrive) at Vienna International Airport at 9 am.
11. Ann and her sister Susan are going to a café. Ann: "I'm afraid I haven't got enough money for a coffee." – Susan: "It's OK, I ______________ (lend) you some."
12. Scientists predict that the sea level ______________ (rise) in the future.

Ben: *"I'm going to keep this skunk under my bed."*
Mum: *"But what about the smell?"*
Ben: *"He'll have to get used to that."*

skunk = das Stinktier

3.3 Future Continuous

Die Bildung

Sie wird gebildet mit ***will be*** + **Present Participle (= Infinitive + *‚-ing'*).**

Examples
- I **will be singing.**
- He **will be walking.**
- They **will be dancing.**

Die **Frage** wird durch **Wortumstellung (= Inversion)** gebildet. Für die **Verneinung** wird ***not*** zwischen ***will*** und den Infinitiv gestellt.

Examples
"Will she be working all day?" – "No, she **will not be** working till late."

Die Verwendung

Die Future Continuous wird verwendet

für eine Handlung, die eine in einem bestimmten Zeitraum der Zukunft abläuft.

Examples
- You will be coming over **this afternoon,** won't you?
- He will be leaving **in a few days.**
- You will be hearing from me **soon!**

⚠ Sie wird vor allem in der gesprochenen Sprache, wenn möglich, durch die Present Continuous ersetzt.

Examples
- You are coming over this afternoon, aren't you?
- He is leaving in a few days.

als Ausdruck einer Vermutung über eine gerade ablaufende Handlung.

Examples
- What will Susan be doing **today?**
- Mum will be preparing lunch **now.**
- Tom will be lying on the beach **at the moment.**

Signalwörter: *later, soon, next ..., at 3 o'clock, then, from 3 to 7, this afternoon, all day long* etc.

3.4 Future Perfect

Die Bildung

Sie wird gebildet mit ***will have*** + **Past Participle (= 3. Form).**

Examples
- I **will have sung.**
- He **will have walked.**
- They **will have danced.**

Die **Frage** wird durch **Wortumstellung (= Inversion)** gebildet. Für die **Verneinung** wird ***not*** zwischen ***will*** und ***have*** gestellt.

Examples
"Will they have returned by tomorrow?" – "No, they **will not have** returned."

Die Verwendung

Sie wird, wie im Deutschen, für Handlungen verwendet, die aus gegenwärtiger Sicht zu einem bestimmten Zeitpunkt in der Zukunft abgeschlossen sein werden.

Examples
- This time next week our plane will already have taken off for Barbados.
- Before long, you will have forgotten him!

Your Turn: 'Future Continuous or Future Perfect?'

Fill in the correct forms.

1. Do not phone me before 8 pm because I ______________________ (watch) the news. You can phone me after 8.30. By then I ______________________ (switch off) the TV.
2. Tomorrow afternoon we are going to meet our business partners from Japan. Hopefully, we ______________________ (negotiate) the contract with them by 5 pm.
3. A: "Could you come round at 5 tonight and bring me the draft of the presentation?" – B: "I'm afraid that won't be possible because I ______________________ (have) a conference at that time, but I guess that I will be able to come round at 8 because we ______________________ (finish) by then."
4. Do you think that anyone of us ______________________ (still, do) the same job in ten or fifteen years?
5. Scientists claim that a lot of species ______________________ (disappear) by the year 2100.
6. A: "By the way, ______________________ (you, attend) the meeting tomorrow?" – "B: Yes, that is very likely."
7. By the time I am sixty, all my children ______________________ (move) out.
8. By the year 2025, we ______________________ (leave) school and ______________________ (find) a well-paid job.

to negotiate = verhandeln
draft = der Entwurf

Aunt Lucy: *"And what are you going to give your brother for his birthday?"*
Iris: *"Don't know. Last year I gave him the measles."*

measles = die Masern

Ziele erreicht?: ‚Future Tenses'

Cross out the incorrect forms to make meaningful sentences.

1. Joanne cannot come on Sunday. She **will help / is helping** her boyfriend to move house.
2. By 2030 I **will retire / will have retired.**
3. I hope **he will pass / is going to pass** his exam.
4. I **will not be finishing / will not have finished** this job before midnight.
5. "I haven't got enough money for a coffee." – "It's OK. I **will lend / am going to lend** you some."
6. This time next year I **will not be / am not going to be** in Austria. I **will study / will be studying** English in Britain.
7. When **will they get / are they getting** married?
8. We **will go / are going** to the theatre tonight. We have already bought the tickets.
9. "What **will you do / are you doing** tomorrow evening?" – "Nothing, I'm free."
10. Do you think Claire **will phone / is phoning** us tonight?
11. She cannot meet us on Saturday. She **will work / is working.**
12. They **will probably be / are probably going to be** on the beach right now.

4 Past Forms

4.1 Past Tense Simple

Die Bildung

Die Past Tense Simple wird gebildet:

1. Regelmäßig: Infinitiv + ‚*-ed*'

Die Endung ‚*-ed*' wird unterschiedlich ausgesprochen:

weich [d]	hart [t]	[-id]
nach stimmhaften Konsonanten [b, g, l, m, n, r, v, w, z, ʒ, dʒ]	nach stimmlosen Konsonanten [p, k, f, s, ʃ, tʃ]	nach [d, t]
Examples robbed, dragged, climbed, rained, cared, loved, followed, buzzed	**Examples** talked, hopped, laughed, washed, hissed, watched	**Examples** added, rented

Besonderheiten

a) Das ‚***-e***' am Wortende **entfällt.**

Examples
- dance – danc**ed**
- die – di**ed**
- like – lik**ed**

b) Bei einsilbigen Verben mit kurz gesprochenem Vokal und bei zweisilbigen mit Betonung auf der zweiten Silbe wird der **Endkonsonant verdoppelt.**

Examples
- stopped
- shopped
- flopped
- robbed
- dropped
- admitted
- occurred
- preferred

c) In der Schreibung enden **Verben auf ‚-y' auf ‚*-ied*',** wenn ein **Konsonant davor steht.**

Examples
- cry – cried
- carry – carried

⚠ **ABER:** play – played

2. Unregelmäßig: siehe Appendix S. 135ff, Tabelle 2. Spalte

Examples
- went
- sat
- came
- got
- kept
- did
- sang
- shot
- wrote
- flew
- drove
- took

Your Turn: 'Past Tense Simple – Forms'

Fill in the correct Past Simple forms of the verbs in brackets.

1. Tom ______ (finish) his homework ten minutes ago.
2. We ______ (come) to Vienna in 2004.
3. When I ______ (be) in London, I ______ (go) shopping every day.
4. Last year my grandmother ______ (stay) in hospital for six weeks.
5. Columbus ______ (discover) America in 1492.
6. Yesterday we ______ (see) you in the canteen at lunch.
7. He ______ (study) French last year when he ______ (be) in Canada.
8. Mrs Jones ______ (break) her right arm in November, so I ______ (take) care of her dog.
9. My first car ______ (be) a Ford, and last week I ______ (buy) a new one.
10. Shakespeare ______ (live) from 1564 to 1616.
11. Last weekend we ______ (visit) our friends and ______ (have) a big party.
12. Some days ago my husband ______ (meet) an old friend from school.

Die Verneinung (= Negation)

1. Sie wird gebildet mit dem **Hilfszeitwort *did* + *not*,** wobei das **Verb** wieder in den **Infinitiv** zurückfällt.

Examples

- I **played** tennis. → I **did not play** tennis.
- She **talked** to me. → She **did not talk** to me.
- We **went** to work. → We **did not go** to work.

2. Kommt im Satz bereits ***was*** oder ***were*** vor, so wird an dieses bei der Verneinung ein ***not*** **angehängt.**

Examples

- He **was not** at home.
- They **were not** ill.
- They **were not** at work.
- I **was not** in my office.

Your Turn: 'Past Tense Simple – Negations'

Negate the following sentences.

Model sentence
They visited their grandparents every week. They did not visit their grandparents every week.

1. She put it on the table. ______
2. I was early. ______
3. He walked to work. ______
4. They went home. ______
5. We were good friends. ______
6. They played football. ______
7. He loved his wife. ______
8. We believed him. ______
9. I visited her last weekend. ______
10. You kept it in your pocket. ______
11. She called them every day. ______
12. The bus arrived on time. ______

Billy: *"Today our teacher asked me if I was an only child, and I said I was."*
Mother: *"And what did she say?"*
Billy: *"Thank goodness for that!"*

Die Frage (= Question)

1. Sie wird wie die Verneinung mit dem Hilfszeitwort ***did*** gebildet, wobei das **Verb** wieder **in den Infinitiv zurückfällt.**

Examples
- I **played** tennis. → **Did** you **play** tennis?
- She **talked** to me. → **Did** she **talk** to me?
- We **loved** them. → **Did** you **love** them?

2. Kommt im Satz bereits ***was*** oder ***were*** vor, so wird dieses bei der Fragebildung verwendet.

Examples
- **Was** he at home?
- **Was** she in her office?
- **Were** you ill?

3. **Fragewörter** z. B. ***who, what, where, when, how*** stehen an erster Stelle.

Examples
- **Who** was your best friend at school?
- **What** was the film about?
- **Where** were you last weekend?
- **When** did you do your homework?
- **How** old was she?

⚠ Fragen nach dem **Subjekt** mit ***what*** oder ***who*** stehen **ohne *did* oder *do!***

Examples
- **Who** went to see him at hospital?
- **What** kept you from coming to our party?

Your Turn: 'Past Tense Simple – Questions'

Change the following sentences into yes-/no-questions.

Model sentence
They visited their grandparents every week. *Did they visit their grandparents every week?*

1. She put it on the table. __________
2. I was early. __________
3. He walked to work. __________
4. They went home. __________
5. You were good friends. __________
6. They played football. __________
7. He loved his wife. __________
8. We believed him. __________
9. I visited her last weekend. __________
10. You kept it in your pocket. __________
11. She called them every day. __________
12. The bus arrived on time. __________

Father: *"Well, Susan, did you get the best marks in your class this term?"*
Susan: *"No, Dad – did you get the best salary in your office?"*

salary = das Gehalt

Die Verwendung

Die Past Tense Simple ist die Erzählzeit für Geschehnisse in der Vergangenheit.

Sie wird verwendet

für in der Vergangenheit abgeschlossene Handlungen, bei denen die Dauer nicht im Vordergrund steht.

Signalwörter: *yesterday, last week, last month, last year, in 1998, three years ago, on Monday, before Christmas* etc.

Examples
- She called me **last week.**
- We went to church **on Sunday.**
- William Shakespeare died in 1616.
- **Last year** we spent our holidays in Cornwall.

für Gewohnheiten in der Vergangenheit.

Signalwörter: *sometimes, always, generally, usually, often, rarely, seldom* etc.

Examples
- When I was a child, I had a lot of friends. We **always** played in our garden.
- I **often** spent my summer holidays at my grandmother's cottage when I was a teenager.
- In winter my elder brother **sometimes** built me a snowman.

Your Turn: 'Past Tense Simple'

Your Turn 4

Fill in the correct forms of the verbs in brackets.

1. "______ (you, be) at work last week?" – "Last week I ______ (not go) to work because I ______ (be) ill. I ______ (have) a terrible cold, and I ______ (have) to stay in bed."

2. Sue and Adam ______ (spend) the afternoons on the beach: they ______ (go) swimming in the sea, ______ (play) beach volleyball and ______ (relax). They really ______ (enjoy) their holidays.

3. "When ______ (you, go) to the cinema last?" – "Oh, I ______ (go) to the cinema last weekend, and I ______ (see) the latest film with Daniel Craig." – "And ______ (you, like) it?" – "Yes, I ______ (like) it a lot." – "______ (you, go) there by yourself?" – "No, I ______ (not go) there by myself. Jenny and Tom ______ (go) with me. They also ______ (want) to see the film." – "______ (they, enjoy) the film as much as you?" – "Tom ______ (do), but unfortunately Jenny ______ (not like) it at all."

4. "Where ________ (George, spend) his summer holiday?" – "He ________ (travel) to Spain for two weeks. He ________ (not stay) at a hotel, but in a B&B. In the morning he ________ (have) breakfast at the inn, and in the evenings he ________ (go) to one of the many bars and ________ (have) some 'tapas' there."

Your Turn 5

Complete the text with the correct forms of the verbs in brackets.

See 'Topics': Social Ties

Jane Austen

Jane Austen ________ (be) an English novelist who ________ (write) about the lives of early 19th century women of the English middle and upper classes. All of her novels were published anonymously.

She was born on 16 December 1775 in Hampshire as one of eight children of a clergyman. She ________ (grow) up in a close-knit family and ________ (begin) to write as a teenager.

In 1801 the family ________ (move) to Bath. Four years later her father ________ (die). Jane's brother Henry ________ (help) her to find a publisher, and her first novel, 'Sense and Sensibility', ________ (appear) in 1811. Her next novel 'Pride and Prejudice', which she ________ (describe) as her best, ________ (get) highly favourable reviews. 'Mansfield Park' was published in 1814, then 'Emma' in 1816.

In the same year, Jane ________ (begin) to suffer from ill-health. She ________ (travel) to Winchester for treatment and ________ (die) there on 18 July 1817.

WWW.BBC.CO.UK – ADAPTED

JANE AUSTEN, 1775–1817

clergyman = der Geistliche

review = die Kritik

Jimmy: *"On the school bus today a little boy fell off his seat, and everyone laughed but me."*
Mother: *"Well done. Who was the little boy?"*
Jimmy: *"Me."*

4.2 Past Tense Continuous

Die Bildung

Die Past Continuous wird gebildet mit ***was* oder *were*** und dem **Present Participle (= Infinitive + *‚-ing'*).**

Examples

- I **was singing.**
- You **were flying.**
- He **was climbing.**
- We **were looking.**
- They **were protesting.**

Besonderheiten siehe Present Continuous, Seite 101

Die Frage und die Verneinung

Die Frage wird einfach durch Wortumstellung (= Inversion) gebildet.

Example

What **were you doing** at 5 pm yesterday?

Für die Verneinung wird *not* zwischen *am/is/are* und das Present Participle gestellt.

Examples

- They **were not dancing** when I arrived.
- It **was not raining** when he left.

Die Verwendung

Die Past Continuous wird verwendet

1. für in der Vergangenheit abgeschlossene Handlungen, deren Dauer im Vordergrund steht.

Examples

- I am rather tired because I was cleaning my flat **all morning.**
- I was working on my project **all day long.**

2. für Handlungen, die zu einem bestimmten Zeitpunkt in der Vergangenheit abgelaufen sind.

Examples

- **At 8 am** Mary was preparing lunch for her family.
- **This time last year** I was studying for my A-levels.

3. für zwei Handlungen in der Vergangenheit, die gleichzeitig im Gange waren.

Examples

- **While** I was learning Latin, Tom was listening to his favourite songs.
- The children were dancing in the living room, and Granny was watching them.

4. für eine länger andauernde Handlung in der Vergangenheit, die durch eine zweite – oft kürzere – unterbrochen wird.

Signalwörter: *while, when, as* etc.

Examples

- **When I was reading the newspaper,** the phone rang.
- **As** we were walking down the street, two cars crashed.
- Pat was playing tennis, **when** it started to rain.

Your Turn: 'Past Tense Continuous'

Your Turn 1

Fill in the correct forms of the verbs in brackets.

1. It ______________ (get) darker and darker, and I ______________ (feel) more and more tired.
2. While the children ______________ (play) football, father ______________ (wash) the car and mother ______________ (work) in the garden. She ______________ (plant) some flowers.
3. "What ______________ (you, do) at this time yesterday?" – "Well, I ______________ (write) some emails."
4. Yesterday the children ______________ (swim) in the swimming pool in the afternoon. Their father ______________ (take) care of them, while their mother ______________ (exercise) at the gym.
5. "What ______________ (they, do) at this time last weekend?" – "They ______________ (have) a party. They ______________ (have) fun, ______________ (dance), ______________ (talk) and ______________ (laugh) all night long."
6. "What happened?" – "When I ______________ (driving) along the river, a naked man jumped into the water before my eyes." – "And did you call the police?" – "No, because while I ______________ (looking) for my mobile phone, I realised that it had been stolen."

Your Turn 2

Nowadays, a lot of people have a Facebook account where they write about their interests and describe what they are doing. Write a few sentences about the activities of your family and friends. What were they doing yesterday at lunchtime?

1. At 12 am my mother ______________
2. My father ______________
3. My friend ______________
4. ______________
5. ______________

A man went to see his doctor complaining of terrible headaches, dizzy spells and double vision. After examining him, the doctor said, "I'm afraid I have very bad news for you. You have only six months to live."
The man decided to make the best of the short time left to him and went out and bought himself a marvellous set of clothes: a fur overcoat, some leather shoes, a suit of the finest cloth, and a cashmere sweater. Finally, he went to the shirtmakers.
"I'd like a shirt with a size fifteen collar," he said. The shirtmaker measured him and then said, "But, sir, you need a size sixteen."
"Nonsense," said the man. "I've always worn a size fifteen."
"Well, sir," said the salesman, "I will gladly make you a size fifteen, but I should warn you that it will probably give you terrible headaches, dizzy spells and double vision."

dizzy spell = der Schwindelanfall

Ziele erreicht?: ‚Past Tense Simple/Continuous‘

Fill in the correct forms of the verbs in brackets.

1. It ______________ (rain) heavily when he ______________ (leave) the house.
2. "When ______________ (you, buy) your house?" – "Well, I think we ______________ (buy) it in 2003."
3. He ______________ (understand) exactly what I ______________ (want) to say.
4. The film ______________ (not be) very good. I ______________ (not enjoy) it very much.
5. I ______________ (meet) Tom at the airport some weeks ago. While we ______________ (wait) for our flights, a lot of airplanes ______________ (take off).
6. When Tom ______________ (cycle) home, a man suddenly ______________ (step) out into the road in front of him. Tom ______________ (go) pretty fast, luckily he ______________ (manage) to stop in time and ______________ (not hit) the man.
7. At 8.30 pm last night I ______________ (have) dinner with some friends.
8. Ann ______________ (watch) TV when the telephone ______________ (ring).
9. Last weekend Paul and Kate ______________ (play) tennis. They ______________ (start) at 9.30 and ______________ (finish) at 11.00. So at 10.30 they ______________ (play) tennis.
10. I ______________ (walk) along the road when I ______________ (meet) Dave. I ______________ (stop) and ______________ (ask) him how he ______________ (be).
11. Jane ______________ (wait) for me when I ______________ (come) home.
12. Tom ______________ (burn) his little finger when he ______________ (cook) dinner.
13. While Jim ______________ (listen) to the radio, Pam ______________ (read) a book. Suddenly somebody ______________ (ring) the doorbell. So Pam ______________ (stand) up and ______________ (go) downstairs to open the door. It ______________ (be) Tom who ______________ (want) to know if Jim ______________ (be) at home.
14. I have not seen Jason for ages. When I last ______________ (see) him, he ______________ (look) for a job.

Mother: *"Jimmy, you mustn't fight, I've told you, you should learn to give and take."*
Jimmy: *"I did. I gave him a black eye and took his orange."*

4.3 Past Perfect Tense Simple

Die Bildung

Die Past Perfect Tense Simple wird gebildet mit ***had*** + **Past Participle** (= 3. Form).

Examples
- I **had talked.**
- You **had sung.**
- He **had called.**
- We **had jumped.**

Die Verneinung

Für die **Verneinung** wird ***not*** zwischen ***had*** und das **Past Participle** gestellt.

Example
- They **had not met** before.
- I **had not seen** the baby before we left.

Die Frage

Die Frage wird durch **Wortumstellung (= Inversion)** gebildet.

Examples
- Where **had he lived** before he moved to London?
- **Had they won** before they stopped playing?

Die Verwendung

Sie wird verwendet für abgeschlossene Handlungen, die

vor einer anderen Handlung in der Vergangenheit liegen.

Examples
- **Before** they had gone very far, they found that they had lost their way.
- **After** we had left, they called the police.

bis zu einem bestimmten Zeitpunkt der Vergangenheit oder darüber hinaus angedauert haben.

Examples
- **By** last December he had lived in Austria for more than sixteen years.
- **When** we first met, she had worked in this company for half a year.

Signalwörter: *when, after, before* etc.

Your Turn: 'Past Perfect Tense Simple'

Fill in the correct forms of the verbs in brackets.

1. We went to Michael's flat, but he was not there. He ______________________ (go out).
2. I invited Nick to the party, but he could not come. He ______________________ (book) a flight to Tokyo.
3. I was very happy to see her after such a long time. I ______________________ (not see) her for seven years.
4. He invited me for lunch, but I was not hungry. I ______________________ (have) a late breakfast.
5. Twenty years after A-levels we went back to our school, but we hardly recognised the building. It ______________ ______________ (change) a lot.

4.4 Past Perfect Tense Continuous

Die Bildung

Die Past Perfect Tense Continuous wird gebildet mit ***had been*** und dem **Present Participle (Infinitive + ‚-*ing*')**.

Examples
- I **had been washing.**
- He **had been shouting.**
- We **had been looking.**
- They **had been jumping.**

Besonderheiten siehe Present Continuous, Seite 101

Die Verneinung

Für die Verneinung wird ***not*** zwischen ***had*** und ***been*** gestellt.

Examples
- You **had not been singing.**
- He **had not been calling.**

Die Frage

Die Frage wird einfach durch **Wortumstellung (= Inversion)** gebildet.

Examples
- **Had you been talking?**
- **Had they been eating?**

Die Verwendung

Sie wird für Handlungen verwendet, die in der Vergangenheit über eine begrenzte Zeitspanne andauern und bereits abgeschlossen sind.

Examples
- He **had been working** for this company for twenty years before he left.
- Jenny was rather tired because she **had been studying** for her exam all morning.

Signalwörter: *for, all*

Your Turn: 'Past Perfect Tense Continuous'

Your Turn 1

Fill in the correct forms of the verbs in brackets.

1. Susan looked tired yesterday. She ______________________ (look) after her grandchildren all day.
2. Lucy woke up at 3 am. She was frightened and started crying. She ______________________ (dream).
3. When I got home, Mike was still sitting in front of the computer. He had just stopped surfing the internet. He ______________________ (surf) the net all afternoon.
4. There was nobody in the room, but there was a strong smell of old smoke. Somebody ______________________ (smoke) a cigarette.

5. She lay down on her bed exhausted. The closed book was lying beside her. She ______________________ (read) for three hours.

Your Turn 2

Combine the sentences with ***after, before*** or ***when.*** Put the verbs into their correct forms.

1. Tom took his dog for a walk. Then he had dinner and watched TV.
2. She banged her head on a tree. The ambulance took her to the nearest hospital.
3. We took the underground to the centre of London. We arrived at the airport.
4. I finished school at the age of 15. Then I started my apprenticeship.
5. They invited us for a drink. They greeted us in a friendly manner.

Ziele erreicht?: ‚Past or Past Perfect?'

Fill in the correct forms of the verbs in brackets.

1. After Tim ______________________ (do) his homework, he ______________________ (go) to the cinema.
2. Before Sue ______________________ (meet) her friends Pam and Ann, she ______________________ (finish) her work.
3. Paul ______________________ (want) to know what Mr Smith ______________________ (say).
4. After John ______________________ (win) in the lottery, he ______________________ (buy) a Ferrari.
5. Ann ______________________ (be) very sad because she ______________________ (not pass) her driving test.
6. He ______________________ (be) late because his watch ______________________ (stop).
7. After the students ______________________ (finish) reading the novel, they ______________________ (start) answering the questions about it.
8. The team ______________________ (play) for only ten minutes when Tina ______________________ (score) the first goal.
9. After Frank ______________________ (do) shift work for a year, he ______________________ (become) a shift supervisor.
10. Sue ______________________ (already, finish) her work when Jim ______________________ (call) and ______________________ (ask) her to go out with him.
11. After they ______________________ (pack) all the suitcases, they ______________________ (call) a taxi and ______________________ (go) to the airport.
12. Before he ______________________ (become) a doctor he ______________________ (study) medicine for many years.

shift supervisor = der/die Schichtleiter/in

The most popular number in the circus was a horse that played the trumpet.
A farmer who saw the horse was amazed.
He asked the trainer how the horse had learned to play.
"No mystery," the trainer explained, "he took lessons for years."

5 Present Perfect Tense

5.1 Present Perfect Simple

Die Bildung

Die Present Perfect Simple wird gebildet mit ***have*** oder ***has*** und dem **Past Participle** (= 3. Form).

Examples
- I **have walked.**
- She **has flown.**
- We **have talked.**

Die Frage und die Verneinung

Die Frage wird durch Wortumstellung (= Inversion) gebildet.

Examples
- **Have you walked** home?
- **Has she flown** to Paris?
- **Have they talked** to you?

Für die Verneinung wird *not* zwischen *have/has* und das Past Participle gestellt.

Examples
- I **have not walked** home.
- She **has not flown** to Paris.
- They **have not talked** to me.

Die Verwendung

Die Present Perfect Simple wird verwendet

1. für Handlungen, die von der Vergangenheit bis zur Gegenwart dauern.

Examples
- We have not heard from him **since** last Christmas.
- She has **already** lived here for ten years.

⚠ **ACHTUNG:** Im Deutschen steht in solchen Sätzen oft die **Gegenwart:** *Sie **lebt** schon zehn Jahre hier.*

2. für bereits abgeschlossene Handlungen, deren Ergebnis in der Gegenwart wahrgenommen wird, insbesondere bei der Angabe von Zahlen.

Examples
- I have finished my homework.
- He has drunk four glasses of whisky.

3. für bereits abgeschlossene Handlungen ohne Angabe des Zeitpunkts.

Examples
- We have been here **before.**
- Have you seen my bag?

4. für wiederholte Handlungen und Gewohnheiten, die von der Vergangenheit bis in die Gegenwart stattfinden.

Examples
- You have mentioned that **every** five minutes!
- She has met him on **several** occasions.

5. für Handlungen in Verbindung mit *today, this morning/afternoon/evening, this week/month/year,* wenn die betreffende Zeitangabe noch nicht vorüber ist, also im Sinn von ‚bis jetzt'.

Examples
- I have read two books **today.**
- Have you seen her **this morning?**
- He has not had any holidays **this year.**

Signalwörter: *already, (not) yet, ever, never, lately, now, till now, up to the present, so far, before, just, for* (Zeitspanne: wie lange?), *since* (Zeitpunkt: seit wann?)

Your Turn: 'Present Perfect Simple'

Fill in the correct forms of the verbs in brackets.

1. Tom ______________ (work) late almost every day this month.
2. You do not need an umbrella, the rain ______________ (just, stop).
3. We ______________ (already, hear) about his problem.
4. Look, it ______________ (snow). All the trees and houses are white now.
5. Nobody ______________ (visit) him since his last birthday party.
6. Oh, what a shame, I ______________ (leave) my mobile at the hairdresser's!
7. ______________ (you, ever, drive) a Lamborghini?
8. We ______________ (see) this film every week since Christmas.
9. Grandma ______________ (wear) these shoes for forty years.
10. John ______________ (just, return) from his skiing holidays in Austria.
11. The children ______________ (not finish) their meal yet.
12. Lucy ______________ (eat) six sandwiches and ______________ (drink) five glasses of wine.
13. I ______________ (be) here for six months.
14. We ______________ (meet) them on the beach several times.

5.2 Present Perfect Continuous

Die Bildung

Die Present Perfect Continuous wird gebildet mit ***have been*** oder ***has been*** und dem **Present Participle (= Infinitive + *‚-ing'*).**

Examples
- We **have been learning** English.
- It **has been snowing.**
- They **have been sitting** in the grass.
- She **has been lying.**

Besonderheiten siehe Present Continuous, Seite 101

Die Verneinung

Für die Verneinung wird ***not*** zwischen ***have/has*** und das **Present Participle** gestellt.

Examples
- I **have not been walking** home.
- She **has not been flying** to Paris.
- They **have not been talking** to me.

Die Frage

Die Frage wird einfach durch **Wortumstellung (= Inversion)** gebildet.

Examples
- How long **have** you **been walking** home?
- **Has** she **been sitting** in the garden all afternoon?
- **Have** you really **been looking** for me?

Die Verwendung

Die Present Perfect Continuous wird im täglichen Sprachgebrauch eher selten verwendet. Sie steht für

1. Handlungen, die in der **Vergangenheit begonnen** haben und die in der **Gegenwart noch andauern,** wobei es sich nicht um eine ununterbrochene Tätigkeit handeln muss. Der **Zeitraum** wird meist durch ***since*** oder ***for*** gekennzeichnet, der Handlungsablauf in seiner Dauer steht im Vordergrund.

   Examples
   - We have been living here **since** 1985.
   - I have been working for this company **for** more than fifteen years.

2. wiederholte Handlungen, deren **Zeitraum bis in die Gegenwart** heranreicht.

   Examples
   - She has been going to Paris for the fashion show **for** the last five years.
   - I have been paying a lot of bills online **lately.**

3. Handlungen, die **unmittelbar vor dem Sprechen beendet** wurden.

   Examples
   - I have been doing the dishes while you were away.
   - You have been working too much, you look tired.

Your Turn: 'Present Perfect Continuous'

Fill in the correct forms of the verbs in brackets.

1. She ______________________ (iron) all afternoon. That is why she has a backache now.
2. He ______________________ (jog) for an hour and a half.
3. They ______________________ (work) all night. Now they are tired and sleepy.
4. He ______________________ (dig) the garden. That is why he is so exhausted now.
5. Dad should take a break. He ______________________ (drive) for five hours.
6. Tony ______________________ (lie) in bed for three days. He has got the flu.

Ziele erreicht?: ‚Past or Present Perfect, Simple or Continuous?'

Challenge 1 – Past or Present Perfect?

Complete the text and fill in the missing verbs.

See 'Topics': Energy and Climate

Some Asian Glaciers 'Putting on Mass'

Some glaciers on Asia's Karakoram Mountains are defying the global trend and getting thicker, say researchers. A French team ________________ (use) satellite data to show that glaciers in part of the Karakoram Range, to the west of the Himalayan region, are putting on mass.

The reason is unclear, as glaciers in other parts of the Himalayas are losing mass – which is also the global trend. The response of Himalayan glaciers to global warming ________________ (be) a hot topic ever since the 2007 report of the Intergovernmental Panel on Climate Change (IPCC), which ________________ (contain) the false claim that ice from most of the region could disappear by 2035.

Although often regarded as part of the Himalayas, the Karakoram Range is technically a separate chain that includes K2, the world's second-highest peak. Much of the region is inaccessible, and there ________________ (be) a general recognition that observations need to be stepped up in order to clarify what is going on.

The French scientists ________________ (compare) two models of land surface elevation derived from satellite observations, for 1999 and 2008. This method ________________ (be) used before in other mountain ranges, but it is not as straightforward as it might sound. "It ________________ (not be) used more because these elevation models are quite difficult to acquire – you need clear sky conditions and reduced snow cover," ________________ (say) lead researcher Julie Gardelle. Having done all these calculations, the team ________________ (find) that between 1999 and 2008 the mass of the glaciers in this 5,615 sq km region of the Karakoram ________________ (increase) marginally, although there ________________ (be) wide variations between individual glaciers.

"We don't really know the reason," Ms Gardelle ________________ (tell) BBC News. "Right now we believe that it could be due to a very specific regional climate over Karakoram, because there ________________ (be) meteorological measurements that ________________ (show) increased winter precipitation; but that is just a guess at this stage."

Richard Black, BBC News – adapted

Challenge 2

Fill in the correct forms of the verbs in brackets.

1. John ______________________ (move) to London a few years ago. He ______________________ (live) there for five years now.
2. I will go swimming as soon as I ______________________ (finish) reading this chapter.
3. Tim ______________________ (not feel) well yesterday. He ______________________ (have) a terrible headache, so he ______________________ (stay) in bed all day.
4. "______________________ (you, ever, be) to Australia?" – "No, I ______________________ (never, be) to Australia, but I want to go there next year."
5. Sue and Pam ______________________ (know) each other for a long time. They first ______________________ (meet) at university and ______________________ (be) friends ever since.
6. Mr Longbottom ______________________ (start) work with this company last October. Since then he ______________________ (meet) several nice people.
7. There ______________________ (already, be) several accidents on this dangerous bend.
8. I ______________________ (learn) Spanish for eight years now.
9. Jason ______________________ (break) his leg in January. He ______________________ (not can) go jogging till yesterday.
10. When I ______________________ (finish) gardening, I will have a shower.
11. This time last month the students ______________________ (study) for their Spanish exam.
12. "______________________ (you, ever, be) to Canada?" – "Yes, I ______________________ (be) there three years ago. I ______________________ (go) to British Columbia and ______________________ (have) a great time there."
13. Tim and Paul ______________________ (not play) tennis for two weeks. Two weeks ago Tim ______________________ (be) on holiday in Italy, and last week Paul ______________________ (have) a business meeting in New York.
14. "______________________ (you, see) the news on TV last night?" – "No, I ______________________ (not have) any time to watch TV because I ______________________ (have) so much work to do."

During school dinner, the teacher asked: "Why haven't you finished your plate?"
"Well," David said. "The peas are as hard as rocks."
The teacher reached over with his fork and picked up some peas from David's plate.
"They seem soft enough to me," he said, tasting them.
"Well, they ought to be," said David. "I've been chewing them for the last ten minutes."

Ziele erreicht?: ‚The Tenses'

Super Challenge 1 – Mixed Tenses

Fill in the correct forms of the verbs in brackets.

1. Look! A spider ______ (climb) up the wall.
2. Yesterday, while father ______ (do) the washing up, mother ______ (work) in the garden.
3. "______ (ever, be) to New York?" – "Yes, I ______ (be) there last August. We ______ (stay) in a luxury hotel in Manhattan for ten days."
4. John usually ______ (get) up at six in the morning, but today he ______ (not get up) that early because it ______ (be) Sunday.
5. I hope the weather ______ (be) fine tomorrow.
6. Sue ______ (do) the ironing, when someone ______ (ring) at the door. She ______ (stand) up, ______ (go) downstairs and ______ (open) the door.
7. The students ______ (have) an English exam tomorrow. So they ______ (study) a lot since last week.
8. After Tom ______ (finish) work, he ______ (go) to the cinema with his friends.
9. At the moment the members of the team ______ (listen) to their boss.
10. Ben and Jenny ______ (move) to Australia in 2005. Since then they ______ (live) in Sydney.
11. When they ______ (watch) TV, the telephone ______ (ring).
12. Granny ______ (be) 80 next week.
13. "What ______ (do) in your holidays?" – "Well, we ______ (not know). I ______ (not want) to go to Italy again as we ______ (be) there last year. I ______ (want) to go to Sweden or Norway, but the children ______ (love) swimming in the sea and playing on the beach. They really ______ (enjoy) it last year. Therefore we ______ (not make) up our minds, but I hope that we ______ (agree) on a destination next weekend."

14. I promise that I ______________________ (not tell) anybody about the accident.

15. "What time ______________________ (the train, leave)?" – "It usually ______________________ (leave) at 6.30, but today it ______________________ (leave) ten minutes later."

16. When we ______________________ (play) tennis last Sunday it suddenly ______________________ (start) to rain.

17. The dancing club ______________________ (have) its summer party in July.

18. Our friends ______________________ (organise) everything before they ______________________ (leave).

19. The travel agent ______________________ (recommend) the hotel which ______________________ (be) renovated last March to the couple.

20. Sue ______________________ (already, finish) her work when Jim ______________________ (call).

21. "Where ______________________ (you, spend) your next summer holidays?" – "My family and I ______________________ (fly) to Spain."

22. Granny ______________________ (not tell) us that she ______________________ (be) ill last week.

23. Mother expects that her children ______________________ (be) at home for lunch.

24. Many people believe that humankind ______________________ (never, fly) to Mars.

25. "______________________ (you, go) to the cinema last week?" – "No, I ______________________ (not go) because I ______________________ (be) there three weeks ago."

26. Since 1990 we ______________________ (live) in the country, but next year we ______________________ (move) to a big city.

27. Many years ago John ______________________ (study) Spanish and French abroad.

28. The secretary ______________________ (just, finish) writing the letters.

29. When I ______________________ (come) home yesterday, he ______________________ (sit) asleep in his armchair.

30. After the children ______________________ (go) home for lunch, they ______________________ (have) an appointment with the dentist.

31. "Since when ______________________ (you, have) your new bike?" – "I ______________________ (buy) it last Saturday."

32. Jason ______________________ (tell) the police that there ______________________ (be) an accident in Park Avenue.

33. Since his wife left home, Patrick ______________________ (prepare) breakfast on his own.

34. Sue ______ (practise) the piano for two hours now.

35. Last night Alan and Jason ______ (go) out to meet their friends. Alan ______ (not drink) anything.

36. Sue ______ (keep, always) us waiting. Why cannot she hurry up a bit?

37. Tom ______ (study) German Literature for four years when he ______ (give) it up.

38. "When ______ (train, leave)?" – "It ______ (leave) at 14.30." – "______ (you, pack) your bags yet?" – "Yes, of course! I ______ (do) it yesterday evening."

39. "______ (you, speak) to my sister yesterday?" – "No, I ______ (not see) her for a long time. I cannot remember when I last ______ (see) her."

40. Before father ______ (go) to town he ______ (clean) his car.

41. Jim ______ (not come) back from his business trip yet. He ______ (be) at the industrial fair.

42. The Millers ______ (buy) a new house last summer, but they ______ (not sell) the old house yet.

43. "What ______ (you, do) when the doorbell ______ (ring)?" – "I ______ (read) a book."

44. The QUEEN ______ (arrive) at JFK Airport at 4 pm yesterday.

45. Climate experts predict that the polar ice caps ______ (melt) in the next decades.

46. He ______ (already, write) six letters, but his sister ______ (not write) one single letter yet.

47. Jack ______ (just, switch) on the radio. It ______ (be) nearly noon and he ______ (want) to listen to the news.

48. While the children ______ (play) in the garden, father ______ (work) in the garage and mother ______ (prepare) dinner.

49. When Ann ______ (swim) in the pool, Jack suddenly ______ (jump) into the water.

50. It ______ (snow) heavily when I ______ (wake) up.

Super Challenge 2

Fill in the correct forms of the verbs in brackets.

See 'Topics': Communication and the Media

Weibo Brings Change to China

The use of social media ______________ (change, drastically) the breadth and nature of public debate in China, but ______________ (it, be) really just a poor replacement for real social change? Beijing's recent floods were quickly followed by the resignation of the city's mayor, as the local government's handling of the crisis ______________ (face) criticism on social media. The incident ______________ (be) a reminder of just how the internet ______________ (change) China.

The main reason for this transformation ______________ (be) Weibo, the Chinese equivalent of Twitter, which ______________ (remain) blocked in China. The country's biggest microblogging service, Sina Weibo, now ______________ (have) 300,000,000 registered users, and ______________ (grow) fast. "Since Weibo, information in Chinese society ______________ (change), it ______________ (become) more transparent, more direct," says Wen Huajian author of China's first microblog novel, Love in the Age of Weibo, which ______________ (be) published via 500 posts on the micro-blogging site.

Mr Wen ______________ (say) sensitive topics like the frequent clashes between residents and local governments over forced demolitions are now widely debated. "Web users ______________ (pay, probably) attention – and often the mainstream media ______________ (respond) immediately, and sometimes the authorities too. In the past this ______________ (be) impossible."

Corruption is another topic, and a number of local officials ______________ (resign, already) after being exposed online.

Since Weibo ______________ (be) introduced in 2009, campaigners ______________ (use) its ability to connect to help street children, boycott polluting companies, even to ban the use of sharks' fins in soup. It ______________ (give, also) ordinary people new opportunities for self-expression, and it ______________ (allow) the inclusion of video and photographic images.

Yet the potential power of Weibo ______________ (alarm, clearly) the authorities. Last year, when a crash on one of China's new high speed rail lines ______________ (kill) more than 40 people, eyewitnesses ______________ (break) the news on Weibo and there ______________ (be) a furious online reaction to the handling of the crisis. Senior railway ministry officials ______________ (resign), and Prime Minister Wen Jiabao ______________ (make) a public apology.

Since then Weibo ______________ (introduce) a new code of conduct for all users, and over recent months a number of people, including prominent journalists and intellectuals, ______________ (have) their accounts shut down, prompting several leading academics to quit the service in protest.

Veteran Chinese blogger Michael Anti ______________ (say) it can bring social change, but ______________ (not pose) a wider threat to China's political system. "So far social media ______________ (have) a big impact on local corruption and ______________ (make) it hard for local governments to shut people's mouths," he ______________ (admit).

He also ______________ (believe) that social media ______________ (give) the authorities a simple opportunity to monitor the concerns of disgruntled groups in society. Social media ______________ (teach) people that "freedom of speech is their birthright".

Duncan Hewitt, BBC World Service – adapted

The Word Order – Die Wortstellung im Satz

Meine Ziele

Nach Bearbeitung dieses Kapitels kann ich

- Aussagesätze in der Grundform Subjekt – Prädikat – Objekt richtig bilden;
- die verschiedenen Umstandsangaben in der korrekten Reihenfolge im Satz anordnen;
- Umstandswörter der Häufigkeit und ähnliche Adverbien an die richtige Stelle im Satz setzen;
- Sätze aus dem Deutschen korrekt ins Englische transferieren.

1 The Basic Structure of a Sentence – Der einfache Satzbau

Im Englischen gibt es in Aussagesätzen eine ‚feste' Satzstellung.

1. Man darf Sätze aus dem Deutschen **nie** mit der gleichen Reihenfolge der Wörter ins Englische übersetzen.

2. Als Richtlinie gilt folgende Formel:

„WER	MACHT	WAS	WIE	WO	WANN"

a) Die Reihenfolge **SUBJEKT – PRÄDIKAT – OBJEKT** ist grundsätzlich nicht veränderbar.

b) Umstandsangaben der **Art und Weise** (wie), des **Ortes** (wo) und der **Zeit** (wann) werden nach dem Objekt gereiht. Wenn am Satzende verschiedenartige Adverbien zusammentreffen, so stehen sie gewöhnlich in der Reihenfolge **WIE – WO – WANN.**

Daraus ergibt sich folgendes Grundmuster:

Subject	Predicate	Object	Manner	Place	Time
Examples					
My partner	prepares	breakfast	carefully	in the kitchen	on Sundays.
A lot of people	watched	the show	happily	at home	in the evening.
Her boss	washes	his car	carefully	in the garden	every weekend.
Susan	cleans	the house	completely	–	on Mondays.
Matthew	is repairing	the TV	desperately	in the livingroom.	–

c) Bei **Verben, die eine Fortbewegung** ausdrücken, z. B. *go, run, drive, fly,* steht die **Ortsangabe** unmittelbar nach dem Verb.

Examples
- He **went to the station** by taxi.
- She **flew to Paris** early in the morning.
- We **went to church** by car.
- They **drove to work** together.

d) Bei mehreren **Orts- oder Zeitangaben** steht jeweils die genauere vor der ungenaueren.

Example 'Ortsangabe'
She met her mother in the hall at the opera in Covent Garden.

Example 'Zeitangabe'
He was born in Dublin at 10 am on April 15th 1958.

e) Wahlweise kann eine Zeit- oder eine Ortsangabe an den **Satzanfang** gestellt werden, vor allem dann, wenn mehrere Angaben im Satz vorkommen. Es kann jedoch immer nur **eine** von beiden vorgezogen werden.

Examples
- **Every summer** the QUEEN has a tea-party **in the garden at Buckingham Palace.**
- **Last night** the jazz singer performed quite well **in the concert at the nightclub.**

Your Turn: 'Basic Structure of a Sentence'

Find the correct word order.

1. many adults | every week | English, German and Maths | study | at college
2. spends | the elderly woman | some time | with her old friend | in the café | on Saturdays
3. to the bus station | quickly | the young girl | runs | every morning | at 7.30
4. journalists | to the press conference | go | at Buckingham Palace | on Mondays
5. a lot of soldiers | in the Second World War | died | between 1938 and 1945
6. several action films | the film director | produces | in Hollywood | every year
7. happily | the cat | every afternoon | on our sofa | sleeps
8. the author | has just presented | in the British Library | his latest novel | in London
9. watches | the young couple | TV | on Saturday evenings | at home | together
10. the athlete | in 2012 | at the Olympic Games | the gold medal | in London | won
11. played | at the concert | the piano | beautifully | last night | Lang-Lang | in the Royal Albert Hall
12. talked | the elephant | quite romantically | yesterday | at the restaurant | to the mouse | after dinner

Vicar: *"You must never fight, little boy. You should always love your enemy."*
Boy: *"But he's not my enemy. He is my brother."*

2 General Adverbs of Time, Adverbs of Frequency and Adverbs of Degree and Certainty – Verschiedene Adverbien

Man unterscheidet folgende drei Arten von Adverbien:

allgemeine Zeitangaben	Umstandswörter der Häufigkeit	Gradadverbien
Sie werden vor allem im täglichen Sprachgebrauch besonders häufig verwendet.	Die Umstandswörter der **Häufigkeit** (= frequency) geben an, **wie oft** etwas passiert.	Unter Gradadverbien versteht man alle Umstandswörter, die ein **bestimmtes Ausmaß** (= degree) oder eine **Wahrscheinlichkeit** (= certainty) angeben.
Examples already, just, now, soon, still, then	**Examples** always, often, frequently, usually, normally, generally, sometimes, occasionally, rarely, seldom, hardly ever, ever, never **occasionally** = gelegentlich	**Examples 'degree'** almost, barely, deeply, entirely, hardly, nearly, quite, simply, totally **Examples 'certainty'** certainly, definitely, possibly, probably, really

Alle diese Adverbien stehen im Gegensatz zum Deutschen meist an einer ganz bestimmten Stelle im Satz. Sie stehen

1. **bei einteiligem Prädikat** (= ‚Present Tense Simple' und ‚Past Tense Simple') **vor dem Verb.**

Examples

- They **already share** a flat, and they still want to get married.
- The woman **usually drinks** some tea in the afternoon.
- The teenagers **deeply regretted** what they had done.
- A lot of my friends **rarely do** sports in their leisure time.
- I **quite understand** what you are telling me.

AUSNAHME: Ist das **Prädikat** eine Form von ***to be (am, is, are, was, were)***, stehen sie **nach dem Verb.**

Examples

- He **is generally** late for school.
- The little boys **are always** shy and nervous.
- I **was sometimes** very unhappy at school.

2. **bei zwei- oder mehrteiligem Prädikat** (= alle übrigen ‚Tenses') **nach dem ersten Hilfszeitwort.**

Examples

- You **will always** remember her!
- They **must frequently** change their clothes when it rains.
- Auntie **has just** arrived at the airport.
- I **will soon** be back. / I **will** be back **soon.**
- We **have already** been to Rome.
- He **had probably** forgotten to call her.
- I **will simply** go and leave him.
- She **should never** have bought this cottage in Spain.

Your Turn: 'Adverbs'

Put the adverbs in the correct places.

1. Susan is a very punctual woman, she is late. (never)
2. Paula and her husband prepare supper together in the evenings. (usually)
3. The children meet friends at Wendy's. (occasionally)
4. The Austrian football players score a goal. (rarely)
5. I have forgotten to inform you about the meeting. (simply)
6. Most people have been to Australia. (never)
7. She has tried Italian seafood. (never)
8. I have a cup of coffee for breakfast. (always)
9. My grandparents eat out. (hardly ever)
10. Granny goes to bed early. (usually)
11. The government will raise the money for this project. (definitely)
12. My mother opens the door to the bathroom without knocking first. (never)

In the clothes shop:
Man: *"Can I try that blue suit in the window?"*
Manager: *"No, sir, you have to use the changing room like everyone else."*

Ziele erreicht?

Challenge 1

Find the correct word order.

1. to their parents | write | a nice letter | in the evening | often | in the garden | the children
2. stayed | I | at the school library | the whole afternoon | today
3. the little girl | the violin | plays | beautifully | in the living room | at Christmas
4. at lunchtime | regularly | buy | junk food | at McDonald's | a lot of people
5. probably | we | will not catch | the bus | in time
6. strawberries | a lot of people | love | in summer | eating | usually
7. in the morning | go jogging | many people | all year round | in the park
8. I | you | think | really | believe | just | do not | you | have | said | what
9. at the weekends | we | to the cinema | go | sometimes | with a lot of friends
10. probably | at work | my car keys | yesterday | I | lost
11. luckily | the bus | we | in time | caught | to the airport | yesterday
12. the Vienna marathon | at Easter | takes place | every year
13. obviously | all these questions | did not answer | correctly | during the lesson | the maths teacher
14. patients | listen | carefully | to a doctor's advice | at hospital | always
15. the athlete | every day | hard | trains | with his fellows
16. the student | has worked | to pass | with flying colours | hard | her final exams

with flying colours = mit Bravour

Challenge 2

Translate the following sentences.

1. George geht jeden Morgen um halb sieben in die Arbeit.
2. Meine Kinder gehen normalerweise sehr früh ins Bett.
3. Meine Freunde spielen sonntags immer im Tennisklub Tennis.
4. Das Flugzeug nach London fliegt jeden Tag um acht Uhr ab.
5. Die Nachbarskinder spielen jeden Nachmittag mit ihren Freunden im Garten.
6. Joan fährt jeden Sommer mit ihrer Großmutter nach Frankreich.
7. Wir laden sehr oft am Wochenende viele Freunde zum Abendessen ein.
8. Meine Mutter liest jeden Tag in der Früh in der Küche die Zeitung.
9. Viele Schüler machen oft in ihren Tests dieselben Fehler.
10. Meine Mutter fährt normalerweise in der Früh mit dem Fahrrad zur Arbeit.
11. Viele Lehrlinge frühstücken oft am Morgen bei McDonald's.
12. Samstags gehen sehr viele ältere Menschen gerne ins Theater.
13. Ich esse regelmäßig in der Früh zwei Äpfel.
14. Meine Familie fährt jeden Sommer auf Badeurlaub nach Italien.

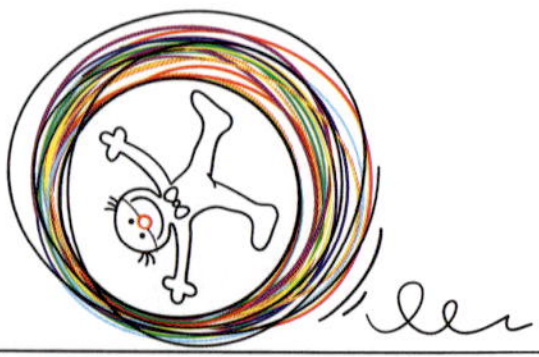

British Humour:
***A:** "I didn't come here to be made fun of."*
***B:** "Oh, where do you normally go?"*

Past Tense Simple

Irregular Verbs – Unregelmäßige Verben

Infinitive	Past Tense	Past Participle	German
arise	arose	arisen	sich erheben
be	was/were	been	sein
bear	bore	born	ertragen, gebären
beat	beat	beaten	schlagen, hauen
become	became	become	werden
begin	began	begun	anfangen
bend	bent	bent	beugen, biegen
bind	bound	bound	binden
bite	bit	bitten	beißen
blow	blew	blown	blasen
break	broke	broken	zerbrechen
bring	brought	brought	herbringen
build	built	built	bauen
buy	bought	bought	kaufen
cast	cast	cast	(aus)werfen; gießen (Metall)
catch	caught	caught	fangen
choose	chose	chosen	auswählen
come	came	come	kommen
cost	cost	cost	kosten (Geld)
cut	cut	cut	schneiden
deal	dealt	dealt	handeln
do	did	done	tun
draw	drew	drawn	ziehen, zeichnen
drink	drank	drunk	trinken
drive	drove	driven	lenken
eat	ate	eaten	essen
fall	fell	fallen	fallen
feed	fed	fed	füttern
feel	felt	felt	fühlen
fight	fought	fought	kämpfen
find	found	found	finden
fly	flew	flown	fliegen
forget	forgot	forgotten	vergessen
get	got	got (US gotten)	bekommen
give	gave	given	geben
go	went	gone	gehen, fahren
grow	grew	grown	wachsen, anbauen
hang	hung	hung	hängen

Infinitive	Past Tense	Past Participle	German
have	had	had	haben
hear	heard	heard	hören
hide	hid	hidden	verstecken
hit	hit	hit	schlagen, treffen
hold	held	held	festhalten
keep	kept	kept	behalten
know	knew	known	wissen, kennen
lay	laid	laid	legen
lead	led	led	anführen
leave	left	left	verlassen
let	let	let	zulassen
lie	lay	lain	liegen
light	lit	lit	anzünden
lose	lost	lost	verlieren
make	made	made	machen
mean	meant	meant	bedeuten, meinen
meet	met	met	sich treffen
pay	paid	paid	bezahlen
put	put	put	stellen, legen
read	read	read	lesen
ride	rode	ridden	reiten, fahren
rise	rose	risen	sich erheben, aufgehen
run	ran	run	laufen, rennen
say	said	said	sagen
see	saw	seen	sehen
seek	sought	sought	suchen, streben
sell	sold	sold	verkaufen
send	sent	sent	schicken
set	set	set	stellen, untergehen
shake	shook	shaken	schütteln
shoot	shot	shot	schießen
show	showed	shown	zeigen
shut	shut	shut	schließen
sing	sang	sung	singen
sit	sat	sat	sitzen
sleep	slept	slept	schlafen
speak	spoke	spoken	sprechen
spend	spent	spent	ausgeben, verbringen
spread	spread	spread	sich ausbreiten
stand	stood	stood	stehen
steal	stole	stolen	stehlen
stick	stuck	stuck	kleben, stecken

Infinitive	Past Tense	Past Participle	German
strike	struck	struck	schlagen
sweep	swept	swept	zusammenkehren
swim	swam	swum	schwimmen
swing	swung	swung	schwingen
take	took	taken	nehmen, hinbringen
teach	taught	taught	unterrichten
tell	told	told	erzählen
think	thought	thought	denken, glauben
throw	threw	thrown	werfen
understand	understood	understood	verstehen
undertake	undertook	undertaken	unternehmen
wake up	woke up	woken up	aufwachen
wear	wore	worn	tragen (Kleidung)
win	won	won	gewinnen
write	wrote	written	schreiben

Practice makes perfect!

Hier können Sie sich noch weitere unregelmäßige Verben notieren!

Infinitive	Past Tense	Past Participle	German

Infinitive

Verbs with Infinitve + *to* – Verben mit Infinitiv + *to*

Infinitive	German
advise	(an)raten
afford	sich leisten
agree	zustimmen
allow	(zu)lassen, erlauben
appear	(er)scheinen
ask	bitten
cause	(veran)lassen
choose	(aus)wählen
claim	behaupten
consent	einwilligen
decide	entscheiden
encourage	ermutigen
expect	erwarten
fail	nicht gelingen
force	zwingen
hate	nicht wollen, verabscheuen
hesitate	zögern
hope	hoffen
intend	beabsichtigen
invite	einladen

Infinitive	German
learn	lernen
like/love	gern mögen, gern haben
manage	schaffen
offer	anbieten
order	(veran)lassen, befehlen
permit	(zu)lassen, erlauben
persuade	überreden
pretend	vorgeben
promise	versprechen
refuse	sich weigern
seem	scheinen
swear	schwören
teach	lehren
tell	(veran)lassen, befehlen
tend	dazu neigen
threaten	drohen
try	versuchen
want	wollen
wish	wünschen

Verbs and Phrases with Infinitive without *to* – Verben und Wendungen mit Infinitiv ohne *to*

Infinitive	German
had better	Es wäre besser, wenn ...
have	(veran)lassen
not have	nicht zulassen
hear	hören
feel	fühlen
let	(zu)lassen

Infinitive	German
make	zwingen
notice	bemerken
would rather/sooner	lieber tun
see	sehen
watch	beobachten

Gerund

Verbs and Phrases with Gerund – Verben und Wendungen mit Gerundium

Infinitive	German
to accuse somebody of	jemanden anklagen wegen
to admire somebody for	jemanden bewundern wegen/für
to admit	zugeben
to apologise for	sich entschuldigen für
to avoid	vermeiden
to believe in	glauben an
to congratulate somebody on	jemandem gratulieren zu
to consider	erwägen, überlegen
to decide against	sich entscheiden gegen
to delay, to postpone	auf-, verschieben
to delight in	es lieben zu
to deny	leugnen
to depend on	abhängig sein von
to dream of	träumen von
to enjoy	gerne tun
to feel like	Lust haben; nach ... zumute sein
to finish	aufhören
to forgive somebody for	jemandem vergeben für
to imagine, to fancy	sich (etwas) vorstellen
to insist on	bestehen auf
to keep somebody from	jemanden abhalten von
to look forward to	sich freuen auf
to mind	sich etwas daraus machen
to miss	versäumen
to object to	dagegen sein, dass
to practise	üben
to prevent somebody from	jemanden abhalten von
to punish somebody for	jemanden betrafen wegen/für
to rely on	sich verlassen auf
to risk	riskieren
to run the risk of	Gefahr laufen zu
to speak/talk about	sprechen/reden von/über
to succeed in	gelingen zu
to suggest	vorschlagen
to take an interest in	Interesse daran haben zu

Infinitive	German
to thank somebody for	jemandem danken für
to think of/about	denken an
to warn somebody against	jemanden dringend abraten von
to worry about	sich Sorgen machen wegen
to be absorbed in	vertieft sein in
to be afraid of	Angst haben zu
to be busy	damit beschäftigt sein zu
to be capable of	fähig sein zu
to be engaged in	beschäftigt sein mit
to be excited about	aufgeregt sein zu
to be famous for	berühmt sein wegen
to be far from	weit davon entfernt sein zu
to be fed up with	es satt haben zu
to be fond of	etwas gerne machen
to be good at	gut sein beim
to be in the habit of	die Gewohnheit haben zu
to be interested in	interessiert sein an
to be keen on	leidenschaftlich gerne ...
to be on the point of	im Begriff sein zu
to be proud of	stolz sein auf
to be responsible for	verantwortlich sein für
to be sorry for	bedauern, leidtun
to be tired from	müde sein von
to be tired of	es satt haben zu
to be used to	es gewöhnt sein zu
to be worth	wert sein ... zu werden
to have a reason for	Grund haben zu
to have difficulty in	Schwierigkeiten haben beim
to have experience in	Erfahrung haben mit
to have no objection to	nichts dagegen haben zu
to have the pleasure of	das Vergnügen haben zu
the fear/hope/idea/thought of	die Angst/Hoffnung/Vorstellung/der Gedanke zu
what about	wie wäre es, wenn
cannot help	nicht anders können als zu
cannot stand	es nicht ertragen zu

Literaturverzeichnis

Black, Richard: Some Asian Glaciers 'Putting on Mass', http://www.bbc.co.uk/news/science-environment-17701677 (15.4.2012)

Gay, Malcolm: More States Allowing Guns in Bars, http://www.nytimes.com/2010/10/04/us/04guns.html (3.10.2010)

Gearin, Joan: Movie vs. Reality. The Real Story of the von Trapp Family. www.archives.gov/publications/prologue/2005/winter/von-trapps.html (6.12.2012)

Hewitt, Duncan: Weibo brings Change to China, http://www.bbc.co.uk/news/magazine-18887804 (31.7.2012)

o. V.: Jane Austen (1775–1817), www.bbc.co.uk/history/historic_figures/austen_jane.shtml (6.12.2012)

o. V.: London Looks to Tackle and Reduce its Mountain of Food Waste, http://www.greenwisebusiness.co.uk/news/london-looks-to-tackle-and-reduce-its-mountain-of-food-waste-2811.aspx (18.11.2011)

Sellgren, Katherine: School Meal Take-up in England on the Rise, http://bbc.co.uk/news/education-18873020 (17.7.2012)

Vaughan, Adam: 'Human Impact on World's Rivers Threatens Water Security of 5 Billion', http://www.nytimes.com/2010/10/04/us/04guns.html (29.9.2010)

Walsh, Fergus: Sedentary Lifestyle Can Kill, http://www.bbc.co.uk/news/health-18880989 (18.7.2012)

Bildnachweis

Urheber unbekannt:

Seite 10 Pub
Seite 22 English Breakfast
Seite 23 Boris Johnson
Seite 72 Maria von Trapp
Seite 79 Logo McDonald's
Seite 102 Pieter Bruegel: 'Country Wedding'
Seite 114 Jane Austen
Seite 124 Karakoran Mountains
Seite 129 Logo Weibo
Seite 131 Covent Garden

Alle weiteren Bilder und Grafiken sind Eigentum der TRAUNER Verlag + Buchservice GmbH bzw. wurden von der Bildagentur stock.adobe.com zugekauft.